# THE LAST TRAIN

# FROM BERLIN

A story based on true events

# CHRISTEL E. HOVERKAMP

This is Real Person Fiction (RPF) based on the life of Marianne Jerke Hoffman.

**All rights reserved.** No part of this publication may be reproduced, distributed, or transmitted in any form or by any means, including photocopying, recording, or other electronic or mechanical methods, without the prior written permission of the publisher, except in the case of brief quotations embodied in critical reviews and certain other noncommercial uses permitted by copyright law.

Copyright: Christel E. Hoverkamp, March 1, 2013

ISBN-13: 9781091377127

First Printing: 2013

## Acknowledgments:

First, I want to acknowledge the great loss of Peter's brother Fred Hoverkamp (John Frederick Hoverkamp). No matter where Peter and I were living, in other countries or back in the States–Fred was always a great friend and had a contagious laugh.

My other brother-in-law always helped us on our boating problems and marine advice–thank you Captain Doug Hoverkamp.

Peter's sister and her husband were always calm and understanding. "Betty" Audrey Wohl, was a godsend even before Peter and I were married. Thank you for your gracious help at the most difficult time in my life.

The late, Major Helen Magoon–I want to thank you for bringing my mother and I to the States and I wish to thank you for all the help you gave us.

The late, Heinz Hofmann, this man saved my life, literally, and helped my family many times. I can't thank you enough.

I am very grateful to the late, Vivienne Kuhrt. This bubbly sweet lady that everybody loved, helped me meet my husband at college.

In Germany- I owe much gratitude to Marga Flemming, who is still my best friend, and to her mother, the late, Maria Loeckher. Special thanks for their special relationship with my mother, the late Marianne Hofmann. Together they created a line of a "Four Generation Friendship".

Dear Peter–Thank you for extending my family from "zero" to all of your brothers and sister, mother and step-father, uncles and aunts, and cousins to our entire family circle. You have made my life interesting, very busy and you have been very loving and supportive to our children, George, Christopher, and Heidi, and seven grandchildren, Asheton, Kelsey, Katelyn, Jacob, Victoria, Emily and Sarah, throughout all these adventures for fifty-three years plus.

Each moment signifies whether an end result is to be good or bad. Trust either develops for the better or for the worse, no matter with whom that moment is shared.

In such instances, decisions must be made quickly, to walk away from them with complete trust in your heart, or walk away with disgust and hope that we can forgive and forget. ~ Christel Hoverkamp

## Prologue

During the latter days of The Great War now known as World War I, Germany was a key player in the original Triple Alliance with Austria-Hungary and Italy. By 1917 the United States had joined France, Britain, Russia and other powers in the war against the Triple Alliance that engulfed most major countries.

A baby was born on 28 May, 1917 in the University Woman's Hospital in Berlin, Germany to an unmarried worker, Anna Marie Nowak, something that was rather frowned upon in those days.

The child's name was recorded as Marianne Marie Nowak. By declaration in April of 1923, Adam Jerke, the girl's father and now husband to Anna Marie gave the child his family name. This was my mother, Marianne Marie Jerke, a tough start that was to be more than a boring life.

Eighteen months after my mother's birth, On November 18, 1918, Germany signed an armistice to effectively end The Great War and the world quieted for a time.

My mother spoke little of her parents; only that her mother had passed away when she was sixteen-years old, and that she, Marianne, had loved her father dearly. She was the oldest of three children, the younger siblings were boys.

After the war and during my mother's childhood in the 1920's, times were lean. Since Germany had largely depended on industry and farming, The Great Depression, which began in the United States, soon gripped Germany as well. The United States could no longer loan money to Germany to rebuild after the war and this dragged the German economy into further decline.

*Marianne and her younger brothers*

Marianne traveled to Poland in 1930 and again in 1931 to visit her maternal grandmother. At the time, Marianne was only thirteen and fourteen years old, proving her independent spirit. She stayed with her grandmother for six weeks on her first visit and eight weeks on her second.

For German citizens, just finding enough food to eat and feed a family was difficult at best. People had resorted to a survival mentality and looked only to care for their own. Life centered on survival and politics were far from the minds of the working class. The country was divided by the very citizens who should unite it. Even a loaf of bread was worth its weight in gold. This was the same throughout most European countries and the people saw little hope.

When Adolf Hitler rose to power in the German Worker's Party, life began to improve at a rapid pace. Food was abundant, jobs were ample and German citizens dug themselves out of poverty. Later, Hitler, the peoples' savior, was appointed as chancellor and transformed the Weimar Republic into the Third Reich, a single party dictatorship.

Under rule of the Third Reich, Berlin developed a sophisticated culture including; advanced architecture, various literature, psychology, philosophy, film production, painting, music and art.

Film made vast artistic and technical advances during the twenties in Berlin, and gave rise to German Expressionism. "Talkies", or sound films, became popular with the European general public, and Berlin produced many of them.

*The University of Berlin*, known today as *Humboldt University of Berlin*, became a major intellectual center in Germany and Europe. The sciences were especially favored. Albert Einstein served as director of the *Kaiser Wilhelm Institute for Physics* in Berlin, only leaving after the anti-Semitic Nazi Party rose to power in the late twenties and early thirties.

Despite the growing culture or perhaps because of it, Germany and Europe lay in political turmoil.

When Marianne Jerke's mother passed away, my mother set aside her dreams to care for her younger brothers and managed the household as her mother would have. She shopped for groceries at local markets, cooked and cleaned and made certain the boys attended school daily and kept up with their studies.

Her father worked hard to provide for the family. The loss of his wife and caring for three children was sometimes difficult for him. Marianne so cared for her father that she rooted herself into the role of the family matron.

Marianne's social life suffered and she lost touch with her friends. Her father, however, met a young woman after a time and soon wanted to marry the woman. Marianne resented her, perhaps because of the attention her father paid to her. The woman refused the marriage proposal initially, due to her dislike for Marianne. One night Marianne overheard a conversation between her father and the woman, and the woman agreed to marry him but only if the oldest were to leave the home. The oldest she referred to, of course, was Marianne.

Rather than cause a scene, my mother vowed silently to leave the house that night. Whether her father defended her or not, she never knew. Early the following morning she packed her meager belongings and left.

Alone and hungry, Marianne wandered the Berlin streets dragging her belongings behind her. For the first few nights she slept in building entryways and once in an alley. She slept little, and ate what she could scrounge or beg from shop owners.

While scrounging food early one evening in an alley, a man

approached her. The finely dressed man was well-spoken and showed genuine concern for her plight. He introduced himself as Reinhold Krankemann and after brief conversation, offered her a safe place to sleep. By now, Marianne was cold, tired and hungry and so, with some hesitation, she accepted.

Reinhold, who had been born in Berlin in 1912 and was five years older than Marianne, led her to his apartment at 47 St. Petersburger Strasse, where she set her belongings in a front room corner. Reinhold prepared a simple dinner while she bathed and oh, the bath felt good!

The two ate dinner quietly. Reinhold asked questions of course as to why she wandered the streets, but Marianne provided only enough information to appease him. Soon, he took the hint and quit asking. After dinner Reinhold left the apartment to meet with friends and told her to make herself at home. He didn't return until well after midnight. Marianne slept on the couch and didn't hear him return.

Reinhold was a handsome man even though he was several years older than she was. He took good care of her, provided her food and made sure that she had what she needed each day before he left for work. Marianne cleaned the house and washed dishes while he was gone, anything to earn her keep. Now that she had clean clothes to wear, she took to the streets in the mornings to look for work, and kept house during the afternoon before Reinhold returned home. After a few weeks their relationship became comfortable. Weeks turned into years and eventually the relationship had become so comfortable that Marianne discovered that she was pregnant.

Reinhold, it seems, was less than thrilled about the pregnancy. Marianne had seen the warning signs in his frequent late night forays out with his comrades, often drinking at the Kneipe (bar), and returning home late at night. The upcoming baby didn't deter his late nights out.

This was a time before birthing in hospitals. Most often women delivered their babies at home assisted by midwives. When I was born on April 25, 1940, rather than attend the birth, my father celebrated with his comrades at the beer festival. Marianne had been unhappy with Reinhold's lack of attention for some time and his absence at the birth of his child set her off.

Mother found work in clerical and as a secretary for the local Railroad authority from 1941 until 1944. This exposure and experience would serve her well in the near future. She had always been a hard worker and between her and Reinhold, they made a good living. Marianne saved and spent her earnings on expensive jewelry and when she dressed up for an evening out, she wore fine fox furs over her shoulders.

Over the following months Reinhold remained true to his nature. He rarely helped around the house or with the baby, leaving the household duties to Marianne. His nights were spent at the local Kneipe.

Eventually Reinhold went off to join the military to fight in what would become World War II. My mother once said that if he returned from the war injured she would stay with him. However, if he returned healthy, he would soon return to his old ways and she would leave him. He did return healthy and so she moved out of the house and took me with her.

It is here that my story with my mother truly begins.

## Chapter 1

As I've grown to adulthood, I've come to realize that most people carry with them the happy memories of childhood. They remember birthday parties and Christmas's with beautiful sparkling gifts. Or perhaps their fond recollections are of family feasts over turkey and ham dinners. The delight of childhood should be to laugh and play, to run in the fields and invent silly games, the rules of which, only the children understand.

Picture of Christel with her doll age ca. 18 months in Berlin before their evactuation.

I have few memories of such things; not that memories of this kind weren't made in my home-city of Berlin. Yes, there were such things, I know because I have heard of them from friends. My childhood however, was different than most.

A lifetime ago I remember living in Apartment #34, Ebeling #9 in a working class section of the city. I recall sitting in our living room early one morning playing with my doll and my teddy bear. My doll's name is Baby Anna and my teddy bear is simply "Teddy." My dog, Roscoe, lies faithfully beside me, watching us play.

The morning seems no different than any other morning until a faint rumbling noise begins. Roscoe barks and races to the window. He paces quickly back-and-forth, barking and barking. "Roscoe, quiet!" I call to him.

At first the noise seems like nothing, and then slowly it grows louder and louder, then so loud that the floors, the ceiling and the walls of our apartment shake. The sound is unlike any I've ever heard. The Allies had started bombing Berlin along with the other industrial, war industry and port locations after a failed attempt by the Germans to level London.

Through the wall I hear the neighbors cry and the cries turn to screams. Mama rushes in from the kitchen looking around the room with wide-eyes.

I cover my ears and scream, "What's that noise, Mama?"

"Christel, come!" she says then snatches me by the arm. I barely have time to grasp the doll and Teddy before she scoops me into her arms. "We have to get to the cellar!" Her voice quivers; I had never heard Mama afraid before, but I sense that she is afraid now. Her fear scares me.

"What's happening?" I ask again.

Mama carries me in a hurry out our apartment door and into the hallway. Roscoe follows on her heels, whining and barking and adding to the confusion. Mama reaches the stairwell and hurries down the steps two at a time.

Other people from the building are ahead of us and behind us. The screaming neighbors follow right behind us though their screams have softened to tearful sobs. Their son, Heinrich, who is four-years-old and about my age, is carried by his father. Heinrich's eyes are blue and watery; in his eyes I see that he is as scared as I am. When his father comes close I reach out for him and he stretches for my hand. Then, the gap between us widens.

As we bounce down the stairs, I can't pull my eyes off of Heinrich. He looks back at me, refusing to pull away his gaze or even blink. Underneath our feet the floors shake and glass is flying and every once in a while I hear loud noises and we hear crashes and crunching sounds. People are screaming: "Bombs! They are bombing us!"

We all reach the first floor, our fleeing group turn as one down the first floor hallway. Mama follows those in front of her downstairs and into the dark cellar. Heinrich and his family follow close behind us. I'd never been in the cellar before but I'd heard scary stories from other children who had.

Other people are already in the dark cellar. Light from high windows shines in from the street. The windowpanes quiver from the rumbling. The noise isn't as loud here in the cellar, but I still hear it.

Mama weaves through the gathering crowd. Roscoe has stopped barking but still whines now and again. We reach a spot that must be toward the center of the building above us since a thick, grey-brick wall centers the large room around us. Mama leans against the wall then looks at me and brushes my brown hair from my face.

The fear is still in her eyes, though she seems less afraid now. "Are you hurt, Liebchen?" she asks.

I shake my head.

She pats my Baby Anna's head. "Good, you brought your playmates. We're all safe here."

"Marianne," I hear a soft voice before a woman steps from behind a large man who I don't recognize. The woman is our other neighbor, Mrs. Schultz who is old enough to be my Oma, my grandmother, if I had an Oma.

The old woman stands close to us, as though doing so shields us from everyone around. She lays a hand on my shoulder and says, "My, oh my, Christel, such excitement, eh?" I nod to her.

Mama says to her, "I'm glad you made it to the cellar. I thought I should have checked on you but we were in such a rush."

"Oh, not to worry, my dear. I can still climb those stairs when I need to."

Mama slides me down and onto the floor. I sit with my back to the cold brick and Roscoe lays close enough that I can feel his body heat. I pat his head softly, "It's okay, boy."

I sit Baby Anna and Teddy in my lap facing me. They don't look afraid. "I'm scared." I tell them very quietly.

I look through the forest of legs standing in front of me. Most people stand still, only a few fidget around though I don't understand why; they have nowhere to go.

Then I see Heinrich's blue eyes looking at me. His hand is stretched up to hold a man's hand. The legs he stands next to look like his father's so I suppose it's his father's hand that he holds onto. Heinrich doesn't look afraid anymore; he looks lost. Just like on the staircase, Heinrich doesn't look away. Then, a few people shift and he's swallowed up in the sea of legs.

Mama and Mrs. Shultz are talking but I'm not paying attention. I wish they would say what is happening. Maybe they don't know or don't care what is happening. I want to know.

The rumble outside continues for a long time. Sometimes the noise gets a little louder, then it gets quieter, and then louder again. Mother talks to a few neighbors but no one says why we have to live in the dark basement now. When we first came down here people talked loud. Now they are quiet, almost whispering like we're playing hide-and-seek. Maybe that's what we're doing and they forgot to tell me.

Baby Anna needs a nap and I'm hungry. I want to go home now.

Then I hear sirens. Not one siren but lots of them and they are louder than the rumbling. I hold my hands over my ears so the sirens don't blow up my ears.

Roscoe barks at the noise and he runs in a circle. I know he wants to run after the siren but he won't leave me. Mama nudges him with her foot and tells him to shut up. She reaches down to me and says; "Okay, Liebchen. Let's go home."

I gather Baby Anna and Teddy in one arm and hold her hand with the other. She lifts me up from the cold floor. The people in the cellar are moving away from us. Maybe we won the game, or whoever we are hiding from found us. Either way, I don't care; I don't like this game.

That was the first time we played the hiding game. We played lots of times after that. The noise always came and it almost always shook our apartment. I got less scared as we played more. I knew what to do, gather up Teddy and Baby Anna under one arm and follow Mama out the door. Roscoe always came. I always got hungry in the cellar so I kept a chunk of bread in my pocket so that if we played the game I could eat while we waited for them to find us. The sirens always told us when the game was over.

Between games, our life went back to the way it had always been. I played while Mama worked around the house. After a while, Mama sold the dog. Roscoe was a champion dog. He had won some trophies and stuff when he went to shows. I heard Mama say she got a lot of money for that dog. I don't know why she wants money; I want to play with Roscoe. I don't get to play with friends often and

Roscoe was my best friend.

After she sold Roscoe Mama took me to a store. A man in the store gave her lots of money for her necklaces and rings and bracelets. I loved her jewelry and don't know why the man wanted it.

When we came home Mama took me to her bedroom and she put all the money in a little red suitcase. I didn't see real good but I could tell there was a lot of other money in that suitcase. Then she locked up the case and slid it under her bed.

It seems that we play the hiding game more often now. We've been staying in the cellar longer and longer before the sirens tell us that we won again. Sometimes the building shakes so bad that dust falls from the ceiling. Two times we had to hide in the cellar for the whole night. I didn't sleep very good.

Yesterday I left Teddy in my bedroom and didn't have time to get him before we ran from the apartment. He stayed in my bed alone and worried for the whole night. He was very happy to see me this morning.

The sun is shining in the window now and it wakes me up. I slept on the couch but I don't know why. I don't remember even coming home this morning when Mama laid me on the couch with Teddy and my Baby Anna. I fell asleep right after because it was still dark outside. The noise was louder last night, and it seemed to stay loud for a long, long time. People in the cellar don't talk as much as they did before and they sound scared when they do.

I hear Mama coming down the hall then she comes into the living room and looks at me. "Good morning, Liebchen," she says. Mama calls me 'Liebchen' sometimes; it means 'little loved one'.

Mama sets two suitcases down by the door that goes out to the hallway. One suitcase is the one with the money; I remember it because it's a red suitcase.

"Morning, Mama," I say and rub sleep from my eyes. She lifts me from the bed, carries me to the kitchen and sits me in my chair at the table.

*Marianne Jerke*

Mama sets a plate in front of me, my favorite Frühstück (breakfast) of toast and plum preserves. I like the toast and jam with a glass of milk but we don't have any milk today; so she gives me water instead.

I miss Roscoe. He always sits on the floor beside me while I eat. Sometimes I sneak him bits of food when Mama isn't looking. She doesn't like that; she says he might get fat. I can't imagine Roscoe being fat.

Next door I hear the neighbor people talking like they are in a hurry. I hear banging and thumping. Out in the hall I hear more bangs and thumps and I expect we might be ready to play the hiding game again. I don't want to hide today because the hiding game isn't fun for me.

When I finish eating, Mama wipes my mouth with a dishrag and tosses it into the sink. Then, she kneels beside me and looks at my eyes.

"Christel, we're going on an adventure today. Would you like an adventure?"

I shake my head, 'no,' and ask, "Do we have to play hide-and-seek today?"

She puts her hand to my cheek, "No, no more hide-and-seek. This is a different game. We'll go ride the train. Would you like that?"

I think I'll like a train ride. I don't see very much fear in Mama's face. She looks kind of excited but kind of scared too. I nod my head.

"Okay," she stands up and lifts me down from the chair. "Find your Baby Anna and Teddy. I packed your favorite blanket in the suitcase."

I run to my bedroom and get Baby Anna and Teddy. When I come back in the living room, Mama puts my jacket on. It's my favorite pink jacket with the fur on the collar. The jacket looks like Mama's fox fur that she sometimes wears when she plays dress-up and goes outside at night.

Mama puts on her coat and then opens the front door. In the hallway the building people are walking past, all of them go one way toward the stairs. Mama picks up the suitcases and hustles me out the door in front of her.

"Now try to stay with me," she says and we follow the building people down the hall and then downstairs. She walks slowly so I can keep up with her.

When we get to the bottom floor, we don't turn toward the cellar but we go out the front door to the street instead. I'm glad we're not going in the cold cellar.

Outside it's cold. Lots of people are in the street, not just on the sidewalk either, in the street! Most of them carry bags and suitcases. Moms and Dads and kids are all going somewhere. I wonder if they are going on the train like us. I hope so, lots of people on the train sounds like a fun game to me.

I follow Mama down the street and we turn a corner and go down a hill. We can't walk on the sidewalks anymore because lots of bricks and stones and wood are on the sidewalk. I look at all of the houses, at least, where there used to be houses. These houses are all torn up.

"Mama?" I ask. "Why are the houses broken?"

She looks over her shoulder at me, "What?" Then she notices the broken houses too. "They're broken from the war, Liebchen. Hurry now, we must get to the train."

I walk faster but look at all the burned and broken houses. Some have big holes in the roof or walls. Others are almost gone except for the stuff that used to be the house.

Mama walks faster now and I have to run sometimes to stay beside her. Lots of people go down the hill with us. The people talk and they sound excited. Excited like nervous, not excited like they are going on an adventure. Maybe they don't know yet?

We walk to the bottom of the hill and turn a corner. I hear the train whistle blow and see black smoke climb up into the blue sky. We walk and walk and walk and walk. Mama walks faster now, so do the other people. We walk some more and I run to keep up.

Mama calls to me, "Hurry, Christel! We're almost to the train!"

So many people are around us! I can't look at them though; I have to watch the red suitcase. I trip on a crack and stumble, holding tight to Baby Anna and Teddy. "C'mon babies, we have to hurry! We can't lose Mama!" I tell them.

I see the train now. A long train and it's moving. Mama nearly runs now. The red suitcase goes back and forth and sideways when she ducks around people. She looks over her shoulder and calls to me, "We'll make it! Keep running baby!"

I pass a crying lady who stumbles and drops her suitcase. She calls to a boy ahead, "Hurry, get to the train! We must get on that train!" Although she isn't talking to me, I know that I have to get on that train too. Oh, what an adventure this will be!

My chest is about to explode because I breathe hard. My eyes are wet from the noise and the running and all of the other people running. I bump into some legs and bounce around but keep watching the red suitcase.

The train slows down some and Mama throws the other suitcase, not the red one, into a doorway. Then she comes and grabs my arm and drags me to the train. The steel train wheels scream at me to hurry up. I try but my legs hurt. Teddy and Baby Anna want to cry because they are tired too. "It's okay," I tell them while we trip to the train. "It's okay. We will rest in just a minute."

Mama lifts us up and onto the train step then grabs the red suitcase and climbs on behind us. Other people wait for me to get out of the way because they want to come on our adventure.

The wheels on the train stop screaming and the train moves again. I fall down because it jerks so hard. Mama helps me up and shuffles me deeper inside of the train.

(** author's note: Thanks to the efficiency and details kept by the Nazi regime, my mother received a Bescheinigung, or certificate on 8th December, 1944 confirming that our rented apartment was destroyed in the Fliegerangriff, or air raid attacks between April, 1943 and July, 1944. When the bombings became too much to bear we left as I have related. This must have been in the summer of 1943 as we will see later, and I was never to return.)

## Chapter 2

Inside the train smells like too much perfume, sweat and old shoes. Lots of people are on the train. Some of them stand in the aisles and in places four people sit in two seats. I'm hot and my clothes stick to my skin. My hair is a wild mess and my legs are covered in dust from running. But, as Mama sometimes says, "The best adventures aren't always comfortable."

Some women sob and wipe tears from their eyes with handkerchiefs. One old woman thanks God for bringing her to the train. A man says to Mama that we'll be safer in the south. I wonder where south is; Mama has never taken me south.

The steam engine whistle blows loud and long and I cover my ears. The train jerks and we start moving but we're going the wrong way! The whistle blows and blows; it hurts my ears. The standing people grab onto whatever they can and they jerk back and forth. The train gets faster and then it slows down and stops. After a few minutes, more people come into our train car and we all move close together to make room. I am jammed between Mama's legs and the hardwood back of a seat that has too many people in it.

So many people are talking. A little man with a black hat and gray hair in the seat close to me says we are lucky to get on this train, that this is the last train to leave Berlin. He looks like an Opa and I wonder if he is.

Another woman behind him wipes her face with a handkerchief. Her eyes are red and I see where her tears have washed the dust from her cheeks. She is a big lady and I don't know how she ran fast enough to get on the train. She is lucky to be on our adventure.

At first I don't see any children but then when I look up to Mama who talks to a young lady, I see a boy up above her. It's Heinrich! He lays up on top where people put suitcases and things they don't want to sit on their lap. I tug on Mama's skirt and when she looks down at me, I point to Heinrich. Mama sees him and pats his head. "You found a good seat, didn't you, Heinrich?" He nods to her but doesn't say anything.

Mother lifts both suitcases into the loft above the man with the gray hair and the black hat. Then, she squats and grabs me under my arms. I hold on tight to Teddy and Baby Anna and she lifts me all the way up to where I can touch the top of the train car. I scoot into a spot between the two suitcases. It's hot up here but at least I see something besides legs. The suitcases are too close so I lie on my back and put my head against the red suitcase and push the brown one with my feet. I push hard! The luggage moves a little, then a little more and finally so much that I barely reach it with my feet.

That darn whistle blows again and I cover my ears so they don't blow up. The train jerks and moves and we start moving forward the right way. The steel wheels screech and groan and then the train slows and stops again. More people get on and soon we are all packed together so that I'm sure I could walk across on top of their heads and not fall to the floor.

We back up again and sit for a while, and then we start to move forward after that blasted whistle tells everyone we're moving. This time though, we go faster and faster and I hear the clickety-clack of the wheels on the track. Finally, our adventure starts!

After their excitement of the train moving the standing people talk quieter now. I lean over the rail of my perch and see more parents lift children onto the luggage carriers. A little girl, down where the train car ends, sits up high with a little baby next to her. The girl is a little younger than me, about three-years old I guess, but she's old enough to play with. The baby is too small yet.

Heinrich rests his head on his hand and doesn't seem to look at anything in particular, just the tops of the heads. He looks sad and a little scared. He sees me looking at him and he turns away toward the wall.

Mama stands below me, the top of her head barely reaches to where I am. Her now golden hair is neatly brushed and bound into a bun and I wonder how she keeps it so neat. She wears earrings and I'm surprised because I thought the man had given her money for all of her jewelry. Then, I notice her necklace and I know she has kept some of her favorites.

Soon I feel the train start to slow down and I look out the

windows underneath Heinrich. The grass and weeds pass by slower and slower until they are barely moving. Then, stones replace the grass and another set of train tracks. We go slower and slower and finally the wheels scream and we stop with a big jerk.

Some of the standing people move to the back of the car and get off. Through the window I see them outside, carrying suitcases and burlap sacks. I guess they didn't like the adventure.

I wish we could get off. I've had enough and want to go home and play with Teddy and Baby Anna. Anna is tired and wants to sleep in my bed tonight, but I think Mama isn't tired of this adventure yet. She reaches up and opens up the brown suitcase. From inside she pulls out a half-loaf of bread and a half-filled jar of plum preserves. My favorite breakfast!

She gives me the bread and the bottle after she opens it. I rip off a chunk of bread and dip it into the jam. Mama doesn't let me eat this way much, but it's my favorite way to eat bread and jam.

Oh my, it's good. The sweet and the salt in the bread make me thirsty. I ask, "Did you bring milk, Mama?"

She pats my leg, "No, no milk baby. We'll stop somewhere soon and get you some milk though. Maybe we'll eat a nice dinner somewhere to celebrate. Would you like that?"

I nod and bite into the preserve soaked bread. Mama pulls out Baby Anna's bottle from her purse and hands it up so I can feed my baby. Teddy doesn't eat though, he never eats. I can only guess he must eat while I'm asleep. I know he eats because he never gets skinny, he's always fat.

The train whistle blows and I can't even cover my ears with my sticky hands. I wince and scrunch up my face to keep the noise away. The train jerks and I nearly fall off the carrier but Mama presses me back up. The whistle blows again, then again and we go faster and faster. The clickety-clack comes back and soon we ride really fast out of town.

The train passes through many towns. I'm tired and my babies are tired. We all want to go home and it looks like the train will never turn around. I don't know what sort of adventure this was supposed to be, but it's not working out the way I had hoped.

By nightfall I'm hungry and we have no food. I lay on the carriage deck, holding Baby Anna and Teddy and I watch the people below.

More people have gotten off the train in each town where we stop than have gotten on. Now, at least, the people have room to stand. The seats are still full and sometimes they switch off standing and sitting.

I wrap Teddy and Anna in my blanket because they are getting cranky. I don't wrap them right, so I do it again. Over and over I wrap them up and each time it's not the way they like to be wrapped up. A man gets up from his seat when we stop in a town and Mama gets her turn to sit. She looks up my way, then lays her head back on the seat and closes her eyes.

Voices wake me up. I look outside the windows and see the early morning light. Mama is standing again. An old woman sits in the seat she had sat in before I fell asleep.

"Mama?" I try to say not too loud.

Mama looks up to me and smiles.

"I'm really hungry. Can we go home now?"

Her eyes look sad when she shakes her head slowly. "We're almost in Nuremburg, baby. We'll get off and find something to eat."

"Okay," I say and wonder if Nuremburg is south. We were supposed to go south to get safe.

The next time the train stops, Mama boosts me down from the carriage place and sets me on my feet. My legs are tired even though I've been laid down. She gathers the red and brown suitcases and people move out of our way so we can get off the stupid train.

I step down the stairs and then hold tight to my babies when I jump down to the stones. The air is warmer here than at our apartment in Berlin. Lots of people get off with us. Mama points and says, "Let's try up that way, Christel."

We head off trying to stay on the edge of the crowd of people who mostly go the same way that we do. Instead of following the sidewalk, like Mama always tells me to, we cut across a small field and then climb a hill and find a street with lots and lots of buildings. A lot of cars and trucks drive on the street and even more are parked beside it. There surely must be a lot of people in Nuremburg to drive this many cars.

We turn onto the sidewalk and walk past a few buildings. Then Mama steps close to the street and looks up at a sign on the building we're standing in front of.

"This looks good," she says. I follow her and open the door so she doesn't have to set the suitcases down.

When I open the door I smell wonderful food smells! Lots of people are inside but we find a table with no one sitting at it. My stomach hurts because the food smells so good! I lay my blanket on an empty chair and sit Baby Anna and Teddy on top of it.

A round lady comes to our table and asks, "What'll you have, girls?"

Mama picks papers from the top of the table and orders us both a traditional German Frühstück called a Strammer Max. I'm happy that I get my own because I could eat ten of them right now.

When the lady brings breakfast, it's a little different than the one Mama makes at home. A Strammer Max has a piece of bread fried in butter, and then you put some swiss cheese on top, a slice of ham and then put two eggs on the very top. This morning the lady added two slices of tomato and a big sliced pickle. I don't eat tomatoes much but I eat these. I eat it all and drink two big glasses of milk. Mama takes me to the bathroom afterward.

When Mama tries to pay the woman, the woman tells her that the money that she has isn't any good. "What?" Mama asks her, embarrassed.

The woman tells her that the money that we have isn't worth the paper it's printed on anymore. I don't know what this means. Mama opens the brown suitcase and gives the woman one of her nice necklaces. The lady is happy to take it to pay for our breakfast. So, then I wonder, what will Mama do with all of the money in that red suitcase?

I gather up Baby Anna, and Teddy and my blanket. Mama seems out of sorts when we leave the little eating place. But, I know my Mama is tough. See, she got tough when she left my Opa and lived out in the street for a while. Mama always knows what to do.

Out on the street we walk down past a lot of buildings. Cars go by and people walk past and my mama doesn't talk to any of them. Then, she sees a building across the street. She makes me hold onto the handle of the red suitcase while we run across in front of all the cars. We go inside of the building that she saw and the inside is filled with old junk. Music instruments, and car parts, big records, dolls and toys all sit on dusty shelves.

Mama crosses the room and sets the suitcases down in front of a counter. A gray haired man with glasses sits behind the counter. He wears a hat that has no top, just the brim shades his eyes which makes no sense because there isn't much light in here. The man is real skinny and I guess he must be sick.

"Guten Morgen, Fräulein." The man says to her.

"Guten Morgan," Mama says to him. I wander away to look at the dolls while Mama talks to the skinny man. She takes more jewelry out of her suitcase, and two of her fox furs. She lays them on the counter and the two begin to argue. Before long, the man gives Mama some new money and Mama doesn't look very happy when she lifts the suitcases and calls to me, "Let's go, Christel. We're done here!" The look in her eye tells me that her call is meant for me as much as it is for him.

When we head back down the street in the same direction that we'd come from, I call to Mama ahead of me; "Where are we going?"

"Back to the train," she says.

"Can we go home now?"

Suddenly she stops. The suitcases hang loose in her hands and her head hangs low. Then, she turns slowly and sets down the suitcases. "Come here, baby." She kneels and holds her arms out to me.

She takes my hands and looks at me serious, like she does sometimes when she wants me to listen carefully.

"We're not going home to Berlin. Home isn't safe anymore. We must make a new home now. I'm not sure how or exactly where, but somewhere safe, alright?"

"But I want to go home and sleep in my bed."

She shakes her head and repeats. "Home isn't safe, honey. We'll find another home and a nice comfortable bed." She stands and lifts the suitcases. "Follow me now; we must get to the train."

Even at such a young age I realize that all I have in the world is my babies, my blanket, my mother and whatever she had packed in the suitcase. We have no home and I don't like the thought of riding on that smelly train again.

We make it to the train in plenty of time. This didn't seem to be the same train; it smells the same but looks different. Not as many people get on and we wait a long time for the train to move. Mama puts up the suitcases. I sit in a seat next to her and cram Baby Anna and Teddy up against the wall underneath the window, wrapped snug in their blanket to nap. I don't tell them that we aren't going home but I know they heard when Mama told me. They are both quiet and don't say anything about it.

When the train moves and we leave town, the clickety-clack of the rails starts again. Mama talks to a woman across the aisle from her and my eyes get tired. I lean over and lay my head down next to my babies. Mama pulls my feet up on her lap and takes off my shoes.

I sleep for a while until the train jerks and scares me awake. The clickety-clack is gone and the train slows down and then stops. Mama brushes my hair from my face and smiles. Then she leans over and kisses my cheek.

"Let's get off and go for a walk," she says. "I'm tired of trains, aren't you?"

I sit up and nod and tell her I'm tired of trains and tired of this adventure.

"Then it's time we find a home," she says.

I'm excited to have a new home but not excited about finding one. To find a new home you have to go and look at lots of homes and then go to more homes and it seems like forever before you find just the right home. That's not fun for me.

A lot of people get off the train with us; one of them is the lady that Mama talked to. Mama hauls the suitcases onto the gravel by the train and I follow with Baby Anna and Teddy wrapped up in the blanket. We pass a sign that I'm too young to read but I try to sound it out anyway. *Willkommen in Vilsbiburg* it says. (Welcome to Vilsbiburg.)

The day is warm and sunny in mid-July. The war had not reached this part of Bavaria yet. (Vilsbiburg is near Landshut and Munich. At this time, Munich was in the process of being destroyed.)

The lady from the train walks with mother all the way down the tracks and up the sidewalk to the street. We go to a parking place and the two haven't stopped talking the whole way. We load the suitcases into a car and the other lady drives us out of the lot.

We drive down a street between buildings. This is different than Berlin and even Nuremburg, this town has hardly any buildings and the street is mostly dirt. It's hardly any time at all when we drive past all of the buildings and out into beautiful green fields on both sides of the road. Tall trees border the fields and most of the fields are surrounded by barbed-wire fences. Sometimes the fences are separated from their neighbor's property by hedgerows. On the other side of the fences are lots of different animals that I haven't seen before. Mama points out ducks and geese, cows and horses and we see some pigs and goats too. We pass one house that sits back in a field and I see a boy and girl out playing in the yard. Mama seems very happy to me. She hasn't been very happy since we started this adventure.

I hold Baby Anna and Teddy up to the window so they can see the animals too. We drive a long way down one road, and then we turn onto another road by a big group of very tall trees.

The trees and grass are so green here. I've never seen anything like this. I want the lady to stop the car so I can get out and explore the grass. I've never thought there is so much grass in the whole world!

After driving for a very long time, the car slows and turns into a small road that winds through a field of very tall, dark brown grass. But it doesn't look like grass because it has little puffs on top. This road isn't very long and we soon come to a farmhouse. The lady parks the car between two houses. The one house is white and looks like a house that people live in.

The other house is very, very big, as big as three houses. The walls are painted red, with a pointed roof and the roof is very steep. The house part sits on top of grey stones that have lots of red doors in between the stones. The top part, the biggest part, has white paned windows topped with white painted arches, and the wall has pictures. Not a lot of pictures, just one, painted three times. The picture is a white circle and inside it looks like a bunch of the grass in the field.

Six kids work out by the big red house. A lady comes out of the white house and comes toward the car. She looks happy; very happy. The lady who drove the car gets out and runs around the car to meet her. They hug and they both look happy. Mama opens the car door and then opens my door.

I gather up Teddy and Baby Anna and my blanket and I climb out of the car. The road is dusty, but there's lots of green grass by the houses.

The driver lady tells the other lady who Mama is, and the lady tells

Mama that it's nice to meet her. Then, she comes to me and kneels down, and says, "You must be Christel."

I nod and then look up to Mama. A man comes over from the barn and a tall girl with long dark curly hair follows him. Mama talks to the man and lady for a little bit. I watch the kids working. Some of them are about my age but most of them are older. Not as old or as tall as the girl with the curly hair though.

The girl comes to me and kneels down on both knees. "Are those your babies?" she asks.

I nod my head.

"Those are pretty babies. What are their names?"

I hold up the bear first and tell her his name. She reaches out for my doll. "And what's this one's name?"

"Baby Anna," I say quietly and hold the baby out for her. "You can hold her for a minute."

"Danke. My, doesn't she have pretty brown hair and beautiful brown eyes, just like you, Christel."

I feel my face get red. "You're pretty too." I tell her.

Her eyes widen and she says, "Vielen Dank," which means thank you very much.

"What's your name?"

Her dark eyes sparkle when she looks into my eyes. "My name is Rosemarie, but everyone calls me Romy."

I nod shyly and hold out my arm to take Baby Anna back from her. She stands as Mama comes to us. Mama drops to one knee in front of me.

"Christel, Herr and Frau Ackermann would like you to stay with them for a little while. Would you like to stay here?"

I shake my head and she doesn't notice.

"Mama has to find work so we can buy a home to live in. This will just be for a little while."

I shake my head again and she stands, then goes to the car and takes both suitcases from the trunk. Romy has tears in her eyes. She turns so I can't see, puts her hands in her back pockets then walks over to the older man and woman. They talk while Mama takes my clothes out from the brown suitcase and exchanges it for the money in the red suitcase. Mama takes the suitcase to the woman by Romy and gives it to her. Then, she takes some of the new money from her purse and gives it to the man. They say some words but I can't hear what they are saying. Romy takes the suitcase from the woman and then comes to me and holds out her hand.

"Would you like to come with me, Christel? I'll show you your bed."

Mama stoops down to hug me. She brushes my cheek with her hand and kisses me. "You be good for the Ackermanns. I'll return when I can."

My eyes get wet. A tear falls down on my cheek because I don't know what she means. Since we left home Mama is all I have in the world and I don't know where she is going. I don't know these people.

Mama takes my hand and puts it in Romy's hand. "Go now. Behave. See your new bed."

Romy and I walk toward the house until we hear the car door close. Then another one closes. We stop and the car engine starts up. Mama is in the car with the driver lady. Frau Ackermann waves to them and the car backs up, then turns around. A dust cloud rises behind the car as Mama drives away down the little road that runs between fields of tall brown grass.

Although I didn't know it at the time, I would see my mother rarely over the next three years, maybe three or four times total. I remember feeling very alone through those years.

## CHAPTER 3

Over the following weeks on the farm I learn that Romy is the oldest daughter of Frau and Herr Ackermann. Her big brother, Viktor, has graduated school and works hard on the farm beside his father, Herr Ackermann.

The night that I came to the house, Romy took me to the barn and introduced me to their dog, Patch. "Patch is an Australian shepherd," she says. Patch is white with big black spots. One of the spots covers his eye, which is why they named him Patch. Patch is very friendly and loves to be petted and to fetch anything that I throw for him. He always brings it right back to me, but not for anyone else.

I learned that the big red house isn't a house for people; it's called a Scheune (barn). We open up the back doors in the morning and all the cows come out. The ducks and chickens run in an out all day. The pigs mostly stay outside in their pens unless one of them is sick, then Viktor or Herr Ackermann puts them in the Scheune.

Viktor's shoulders are broad and he is as strong as a boy his age can be, I imagine. I sometimes see him carry a bale of hay in each hand to feed the cows. Though he is mostly quiet, he likes to laugh loud and laughs easily.

I first heard his laugh when one of the farm geese chased me across the grass by the barn. That morning Romy had put a yellow ribbon in my hair that had come loose and dangled down my back. The goose had tried to grab it. Viktor came to my rescue and snatched the goose by a leg and set it off behind the barn where it wouldn't bother me. When he returned, he knelt by me and told me that if it happened again that I was to stand up to that old goose and not run from him. I told him I never wanted to see that goose again, and that's when he laughed. I knew then that I'd be safe as long as Viktor is here to look out for me.

I sit on a hay bale in the barn loft while Viktor brings the cows in for milking. Patch sits next to me and I pet him while I watch Viktor work. Dim evening light comes in the barn door and windows. I like sitting here in the barn when the work is done and Romy and Frau Ackermann fix our dinner.

Viktor looks up to me from the barn floor and asks, "Are you tired, Sprite?"

"What's a Sprite?" I ask him.

He smiles wide and breaks a bale to feed the cows. "A Sprite is a little fairy. They're very magical."

"You worked hard today," he adds.

"You work hard too," I tell him.

"Hard work is good. I like work, it keeps me strong."

Christel on Ackermann's Farm, in Vilsbiburg, ca 1945.

I simply nod and don't answer. He grabs a rope hanging from a nail on the wall and asks, "have you ever ridden a cow?"

I tell him, "People don't ride cows."

Viktor laughs loud, "But Sprites do, sometimes." He motions for me to come down as he wraps the rope around a black and white spotted cow. The cow's udder bulges with milk; she looks uncomfortable. "Bessie likes to be ridden."

I make my way down from the loft and Viktor lifts me onto her back. Since the cow has no hair like a horse's mane to grip, Viktor holds my hand so that I don't fall off. The cow is bony and not very comfortable. I move my bottom around to find just the right spot between her bones where it fits me.

Then he says, "Hold tight, we'll go slow."

He leads the cow with me on top out of the barn and out into the field. Patch runs into the field ahead of us looking for rabbits. I sway back and forth with each footstep from the cow. Viktor's hand is very strong and he keeps me balanced.

The sun sets over the distant tree lined hills. The clouds are yellow and orange with a little bit of red. The breeze pushes my hair back from my shoulders. When we reach the far end of the field I notice yellow wild flowers that I hadn't seen before. I study Viktor's broad shoulders and his strong legs while he leads the cow.

Viktor turns his head a little and asks, "Are you happy on our farm?"

"Pretty happy," I tell him. "We always have lots of work to do. I like the animals and all the green grass. And I like playing with Patch."

"Is there no grass in Berlin?"

He makes me giggle, "Not very much; just in little places sometimes in front of houses."

"Did you live in a house?"

"No, we lived in an apartment. Our building had lots of apartments and no grass."

Viktor stops the cow and stands next to me. I sit quietly as the last sunlight fades into night. Far from city lights, the stars shine above. The clouds hold the glow as long as they can before giving into the darkness.

"Someday maybe I'll go to Berlin," Viktor says.

"You will like it. Berlin has lots of good food."

"What's your favorite to eat?"

It doesn't take me long to answer, "Cinnamon buns; big fat ones with icing on top. They are SO good!"

He pats my leg, "Well, when I go to Berlin, I'll eat a fat cinnamon bun and think of you."

He suddenly seems to remember his work and turns the cow toward the barn. "We'd better get back. Now you can tell everyone that you've ridden a cow, Sprite."

I hold Viktor's hand tight while the cow turns and plods back toward home. It seems to me that no matter how hard Viktor works, he always walks straight and tall and never looks tired. We return to the barn and Viktor boosts me down from the cow. He holds her while I pat her head. I climb back to the loft to let Viktor begin milking. Patch jumps up the hay bales to sit beside me. As I sit and watch Viktor, I realize that I'm happy for the ride. This happy is different though. Mostly when I'm happy I laugh and run and play; this is a quiet happy.

Romy's younger sister, Letta, is eleven years old. Like Romy she is lean and brown curly hair tumbles over her shoulders. She doesn't have Romy's beauty though I think she might get it when she grows as tall as Romy.

The Ackermann's youngest child, Karl, has his older brother's platinum hair and blue eyes. He often follows Viktor around and works hard. I think Karl will grow up to look just like Viktor.

Karl likes to tend the garden mostly. He and Frau Ackermann spend hours in the garden almost every day. They grow corn and tomatoes, cabbage, lettuce, carrots, onions and garlic and beets. I don't like beets too much but always eat everything Frau Ackermann cooks. In one big corner Frau Ackermann grows flowers. Sometimes I go in and she lets me smell them and tells me their names.

Other children live on the farm; children like me whose mothers and fathers try to survive the war. Minna is closest to my age and will soon have her fourth birthday. Minna misses her Mama a lot and she cries herself to sleep every night. This worries me because she sleeps in the same room as me. I talk to her and tell her it's all right and that I miss my mama too. Romy often lies in her bed and holds her until she falls fast asleep. Most nights Romy falls asleep there too and doesn't wake up till morning. Minna's sadness makes me want to cry.

Minna's small bed sits in the corner, then my bed in the center of the room and Ingrid's bed nearest the door. Ingrid is seven years old, blonde, quiet and a very hard worker for her age.

Some nights Patch lies by my bed while Romy reads stories from a big book. My favorite is Hansel and Gretel about a little boy and girl who are a little older than me. Their wicked step-mother takes them deep into the woods and leaves them there. But they are too smart for her and always find their way home, that is, until they meet a wicked witch.

My other favorite story is called, Käthchen and the Kobold, an old German folk tale about a girl, and an imp. An imp is kind of like a fairy and it reminds me of Viktor calling me "sprite". Imps are very magical and the story makes me feel good.

Boris sleeps in Viktor's room. Boris is seven years old and he's round. His face is round, his tummy is round and his legs are big. He doesn't work hard. He hides sometimes while the rest of us do the work. I once saw him eat a bug and his nose is always runny. I don't like Boris because he's lazy.

When I get up in the morning, Frau Ackermann always cooks Frühstück for all of us kids. My favorite is the fresh eggs that Romy and I gather every day from the chickens. We always have eggs and bacon or ham from the pigs. Sometimes we have fried potatoes too and I like those a lot. Frau Ackermann is a good cook. We never run out of milk because we have six cows and two calves. Mama would like this because she wouldn't need to buy milk at the market.

Twice a week in the early morning, Ingrid and Letta take some milk from the cows and pour it into a big round Topf (crock). They cover it and let it sit in a cool place in the barn for most of the day. Before nighttime comes, they go to the barn and lift off the lid, then scoop cream from the top of the milk. The cream goes into a butter churn, that's a wooden barrel on a stand. The barrel has a handle that they turn and turn for a long time. When they turn the handle, the barrel spins round and round. Then, when they stop and take the top off, they pour out delicious buttermilk and scoop out fresh, creamy butter.

On the days when Letta and Ingrid churn the butter, Frau Ackermann usually makes bread or biscuits with our supper. It tastes so good with the butter.

After Frühstück, Romy and I let the cows out of the Scheune and then we throw grain out for the chickens and the ducks. Patch follows behind the cows to make sure they go all the way out in the field before he comes back to be with us.

Then we give grain to the pigs. Do you know that pigs will eat almost anything? Chickens too, they're disgusting but I like that they give us lots of eggs.

Minna stays in the house with Frau Ackermann all day but sometimes comes out to play after supper when the work is done. She isn't very happy and I try to play some games that she likes. Romy stays pretty close to watch over us; I think she has to watch Minna more than me but it's nice to know she's around.

After a time, Minna's mama comes to the farm to take her home. She is very happy to see her mama and I am happy for her, though I wish my mama would come to take me to our new home.

Three days later, Boris' mama comes and picks him up. I am happy to see him go because he never helped us much.

The next week three more kids come to live with us. Dieter and Franz are brothers and they come the same day. Dieter is twelve and Franz is fourteen. Both boys are big and strong.

The next day Sabine comes to stay with us. She is to sleep in Minna's bed but I think the bed might be a little small for her. Sabine is six-years old. Her shiny blonde hair goes all the way down her back and it's the same color as Viktor's hair. I like her right away because she smiles a lot and she talks to me.

Two months after Sabine comes I wake up in the morning and everyone in the house is very sad. I don't know why they are sad. We eat eggs and ham and biscuits and no one talks much. After breakfast Viktor comes out of his bedroom carrying a big sack. I know the sack is heavy because his muscles get hard when he lifts it up on his shoulder. Frau Ackermann kisses his cheek and hugs him for a long time.

Viktor tousles each child's hair, says their name and tells them goodbye until he comes to me. He roughs up my hair, then lifts me from my chair and hugs me big. He looks at me and says, "I'll miss you most of all, Sprite. You'll take care of Bessie for me, right?"

I ask, "Where are you going?"

"Oh, I'm off for a grand adventure. I'll go to Berlin and eat a cinnamon bun and think of you. Not to worry, I'll return before you know it." He sets me back in my chair, and his voice gets kind of funny when he says, "don't forget to take care of the cows."

"I won't," I tell him.

Viktor goes outside and puts the big sack in the back of a truck. Herr Ackermann gets into the truck too and then they drive down the road through the wheat field. Romy has wet eyes and her mama too as they wave goodbye to the truck driving away.

Finally Romy nods to me and says, "C'mon, Christel, those cows need to get to pasture."

Patch follows us when we go out back of the barn and open the doors to let the cows out. We throw the grain to the chickens and the ducks, and give the pigs some food. Then we walk into the barn to shovel out the cow pens. Lazy Patch lays down on the hay bales and watches us work.

Romy doesn't say much, so I ask, "Why are you sad, Romy?"

She leans on the handle of a pitchfork and looks at me strangely. She swipes her hand across her forehead and then sits on a hay bale. She pats the hay and says, "Come and sit...take a break." Patch hops across the bales to lay down beside her.

When I sit, she says, "Viktor is gone. He'll be away for a very long time."

"Where did he go?"

"Well..." she stops for a minute. "He's gone to the train. He will travel a long way from home to fight in the war. Do you know what the war is?"

I nod and say, "The war breaks houses."

She looks at me curiously. "A war is very sad. War is when lots of people fight and some people get hurt. Some even die."

"Are you scared that Viktor might get hurt?"

She whispers, "Yes, I'm afraid he might get hurt."

"Will the war come here?"

"No," she says. "I hope not."

I pat her on the knee. "Don't worry. Viktor is very, very strong. He's going to Berlin to eat a cinnamon bun and he won't let the war come here. Viktor will take care of the other men that fight; that's how Viktor is. He will come back soon."

Patch whines and that makes her smile. I think Patch knows when people are sad.

Romy wipes a tear that starts to fall down her cheek and she laughs a little bit. "Thanks, Christel. You're a saint."

"What's that mean?"

She laughs again and this time it sounds good. "Christel is another name for Christina, it means Saint. A saint is a very good person."

Romy makes me feel good, always. Life on the farm would have been hard without her as my friend. We start working again shoveling the poop out of the cow pens. The smell is strong but gets worse when the sun gets hot outside so we always finish before it does.

When we finish, we put the shovels and pitchfork away. We leave the barn and Romy puts her arm around my shoulder as we walk toward the wheat field. Patch romps in the field around us. We can always tell where he is because the top of the hay moves when he runs.

We wave to Herr Ackermann who drives back up the road.

"School starts in two weeks," Romy says.

"Can I go to school?" I ask her.

"Yes, you can. It's time you started school and this will be my last year before I graduate."

I ask, "Did you go to school a lot?"

"Yes, a whole lot. School is fun but it's also hard work. You will like it; you'll meet lots of new friends."

The next day Romy wakes me up early for Frühstück. When I get to the kitchen, Romy and Frau Ackermann have cooked a huge breakfast! Lots of people are outside and they have brought big machines. Some are tractors, I know because Herr Ackermann has one in the barn that he drives sometimes. Some of the other machines I don't know what they are but some are bigger than the tractors.

Men, women and children all come and go from the house, getting their morning meal from the kitchen. Romy and Frau Ackermann are busy serving them. Romy fixes me a plate and sets it on the table for me. I eat fast because I don't want anyone to come and eat my eggs and bacon. The toast is warm. The fresh churned butter melts and dribbles down my chin. This makes Romy laugh and she wipes my chin off with a towel. As always Patch sits on the floor by my chair hoping I'll drop something for him. Sometimes I do on purpose.

The other kids that live with us are gathered around the table eating as fast as I am. Ingrid asks, "So what do you want us to do today, Mama?"

Frau Ackermann stirs a pot of something on the stove and answers; "Help the men where you can. Why don't you, Christel and Letta get the wagons from the barn? Find some buckets and you can take water out to the field."

"Can I help them too?" Sabine asks.

Frau Ackermann smiles. "Yes, that would be nice for you to help too, Sabine."

After we eat, we make our way through the men and machines and go out to the barn. We find two red wagons stored in the back of the barn. The four of us dust them off, and then find two buckets for each of the wagons and put them inside.

I pull one wagon and Sabine pulls the other over to the water pump. Patch follows me the whole time wondering what we are doing. The pump has a handle and if you put the handle all the way up, then push it down enough times, water comes out. When the water comes out though, Patch pushes me aside to drink the water. I shoo him away so Sabine and I can fill the buckets. Sabine and I aren't big enough to pump the water so Ingrid pumps it. Ingrid puts just enough water into each bucket that we can put our hands in and rinse out all of the dirt and dust.

Before we finish the buckets, the men start up the tractors and machines and they drive to the wheat field. Herr Ackermann goes to the barn and pretty soon he drives the tractor out of the barn and follows to the field.

"We'd better hurry!" I tell the other girls. "The men might get thirsty before we get there!"

"They'll be alright for a little bit," Letta says.

Ingrid pumps water to fill the buckets and when she gets tired, Letta takes over on the pump handle. Sabine and I go into the house and get as many cups as Frau Ackermann can find. Romy helps us carry them outside to put in the wagons.

When the buckets are full and the cups are all stacked in the wagons, Romy kneels in front of us and tells us, "Now remember, don't get too close to the tractors and the binders. Those machines are dangerous and the men won't have time to look out for you. So be very careful."

"We will," Ingrid tells her.

Romy's warning scares me and I know I'll have to watch out for the machines. The four of us girls set off for the field, pulling the wagons too fast and water slops this way and that. We slow down to keep as much water in the buckets as we can. The road is dusty and dry and I worry about getting too much dust in the water for the men to drink.

We stay on the road for as far as we can before we turn off into the field for the nearest tractor. One tractor has only gone a little way from the house. The others though are at different places way across the fields! I see this won't be an easy day.

Letta and I park the wagon at the edge of the field nearest the first tractor. We won't go closer because Romy warned us not to. Patch stays with us while Ingrid and Sabine pull their wagon to a path leading toward the far end of the field.

Letta, Patch and I stand for a very long time watching the men work. The tractor drives back and forth across the field cutting down the wheat. Men rake the wheat into neat and straight rows, all the time trying to keep up with the cutting tractor. The men work very fast but a lot of wheat is still in Herr Ackermann's field.

After a while the men stop all the machines in a little group and come over to drink some of our water. They drink and drink and scoop water out and dump it over their heads and wash their faces with it. When they finish, two buckets of water are all gone! Letta and I just stand and stare as they walk back to the machines. Then Letta stares down into the buckets like she can't believe that they are empty. Then, she says, "I guess we have to go get more."

All morning Letta, Ingrid, Sabine and I haul buckets of water to the fields. Patch follows me faithfully no matter how much he pants. On the next trip, Letta and I go to the far field while Ingrid and Sabine pull to another corner to deliver water to the men they hadn't reached on their first trip. Dieter and Franz work with the men on the very farthest corner of the field. They are sweaty and dirty and red faced on our first trip to bring them water. They get worse as the day goes on.

The visiting women and children cart sandwiches out to the men at midday. We hold a sandwich to eat in one hand while pulling wagons of water across the fields.

By mid-afternoon, the nearest tractor had cut deep into the center of the field making our walk longer each time. The tractors across the field however come closer and closer, so the pull gets easier. I have never seen anyone drink so much water! No matter how little water we spill from the buckets, they drink all that we bring every time.

On our longest pull out to the far corner we come out of the wheat to where the men had cut and see the machines have all stopped working. The men all stand in a circle and they yell for us to hurry. They must be really thirsty to be waiting for us!

A man runs across the field toward us. Patch jumps right in front of me and barks at the man. I tell him to be quiet.

The man grabs a filled bucket from the wagon and jogs back to where the other men are gathered. We pull the wagon over the bumpy rows and see someone lying on the ground between all of the men.

Letta drops the wagon handle and we both run to see what has happened.

Franz lays on the ground and boy, is his face red! The man with the bucket scoops out water and puts it on his face and neck. Franz's hand is bleeding and another man tears off a part of his shirt and wraps up his hand. Franz doesn't look very good.

After a while the men lift Franz up from the ground. His knees shake and he leans against another man so he won't fall down. The bandage on his hand is soaked with blood but his face starts to look better. He drinks cups and cups of water before the man who had held him up helps him walk back across the field toward the house. The rest of the men drink all the water we had brought. When they start up the machines, Letta and I pull the wagon back across the field to refill the buckets.

Each time Letta and I return to the pump we drink cups of water because it's hot and we're very dirty. Patch drinks as much as the both of us, then stops by the barn to go to the bathroom. We take a short break and go inside the house to check on Franz.

Franz sits at the kitchen table. Romy holds his hand against the table while Frau Ackermann sews up a cut on his hand with a needle and thread. Franz bites down on a wooden spoon every time she pokes the needle in his skin. He tries not to cry but tears still run down his cheeks.

Romy looks over and sees me watching. "Christel, go outside honey," she says.

I leave the house. I'm hot, my stomach hurts and I feel bad for Franz. Pretty soon Ingrid and Sabine come back with their wagon and I tell them that Franz is in the house and that he got hurt. Sabine asks, "Is he hurt bad?"

I tell her that Franz cut his hand and Frau Ackermann is sewing him up, but I don't think he'll die. Ingrid just shakes her head and starts pumping water into the buckets.

We haul water and the men work until the sun starts to go down behind the hills. The wheat is all cut down and the men bring the tractors in from the fields. Frau Ackermann, Romy and some of the visiting women have dinner prepared inside.

In the driveway between the house and the Scheune, the men make tables out of long and wide pieces of wood, stacked on sawhorses and barrels. Everyone brings out chairs, small tables, cut logs, anything that a person can sit on. The women drape tablecloths over tables and use sheets when they don't have enough. Herr Ackermann and two other men stack a large pile of wood right in the car turnaround place, then they set it on fire!

Women and children shuttle the food and kitchenware out to the tables and soon everyone sits at a table. Before we all start to eat, Herr Ackermann stands up at the head of the biggest table.

"Ich bin Ihnen sehr dankbar," he begins, (which means I'm thankful for you.) "my many friends for helping with the wheat harvest. Though this is a long standing tradition among us neighbors, I feel blessed every time we get together." He raises a stein, "With the good Lord's grace, may this be the best harvest year ever for all of us."

Everyone raises a glass and some call out "hear, hear!" or some other form of agreement.

I sit beside Romy and Sabine sits on the other side. Patch sneaks under the table and sits right by my feet. Franz and Dieter sit across the table and down a few seats. Franz's hand is bandaged with a white clean cloth. He looks no worse for the accident.

Hungry people begin to pass dinner around. First, a platter filled with Rouladen Hausfrauenart, long thin slices of beef wrapped with onions, mustard, and bacon, browned and then roasted. Next a bowl of little boiled potatoes, gravy, bowls of cooked cabbage and fresh lettuce. A heaping bowl of Typisch Schwäbisch (Lentils, Frankfurter and Spatzle) follows next.

Men pour beer from a large wooden keg and the children drink glasses of milk. Everyone talks a lot and laugh even more. I eat until I'm stuffed. While we eat dinner, Romy's attention is fixed on a boy who sits across from her. The boy is quite handsome with dark hair and eyes the color of the sky. He has a bright smile and broad shoulders and looks at her in a way that I've never seen anyone look at another person before. He seems happy to talk to her.

The people eat and eat until almost all of the food is gone. Everyone helps gather up the dishes, pots and silverware and everything goes back into the kitchen. The women work inside to clean up while the men sit outside, drink beer and keep an eye on the children.

The fire has burned down to coals now and Herr Ackermann

throws more wood on top. The women come outside when they finish cleaning. An older teen-aged girl goes to her family truck and brings back an accordion. I'd never seen an accordion before and it looks beautiful to me. Soon another boy retrieves a fiddle from their car; another brings a bumbass, (a single-string fiddle made from a bloated and dried animal bladder.) Women bring in bells and an Opa blows into a Marktsackpfeife (a form of bagpipe).

The sky is clear. The firelight reflects off of the Scheune and the house and lights up most of the yard. The makeshift band plays song after song. I think they have played together at these harvest dinners before. The setting is so new to me, field after field and forests in the distances, barns and then farm houses, which makes this so special even to small children who are happy and content to run and play.

Romy sees my eyelids begin to close. She pulls me over onto her lap and holds me in her arms. I rest my head against her chest and let the music and singing put me to sleep.

## Chapter 4

The train whistle blows loud and soon the clickety-clack of the wheels settle into a gentle rhythm. As the train travels to Berlin in the summer of 1943, Marianne struggles to lift the lone suitcase onto the luggage rack before she settles into a seat.

The train car is all but empty since most travelers ride the train to the south. This train is northbound.

Eight passengers are scattered about in the seats. Only one elderly couple sits together, the rest have found seats to themselves. A rugged and burly young man sits two rows in front of her. His neat cut hair and clean-shaven face hint that he might be off to join the armed forces.

A middle-aged man seated across from the clean-shaven man is dressed in a heavy coat and a short brimmed cap. He sits quietly while watching the German countryside pass outside the window.

The elderly couple sits close in the seat, leaving enough room for an additional person should the need arise. Their dress and closeness tells of a couple who has been together through a lifetime of struggle.

Marianne settles her head against the seatback and her thoughts turn to her daughter back on the farm. She had kept a brave face when she had left her daughter with people she hadn't known before today. Now, a knot welled in her stomach.

Marianne had learned to read people years ago when she had lived on the streets. Some people were to be trusted, others were not. No matter a person's appearance, or what they might say, the trustworthy display a quiet honesty in their eyes that is nearly impossible to fake. She had learned the hard way and now relied on the look in the eye when needed. She felt confident in the honesty and trust of the Ackermanns, leaving them to raise her only child, at least for a time. Still, in the past, her misplaced trust might have put her in peril, never someone else. Certainly she had never before considered trusting anyone with her daughter. But, she justified in her mind, these were desperate times. She sensed that the coming weeks and months would present opportunities she would have never considered before. She felt up for the challenge, after sleep; only after sleep.

Marianne closed her eyes. The rocking train car and tapping wheels sung her to sleep. The sun set, dousing the car in darkness save for a few dim lights along the bulkhead.

*Marianne Krankemann*

When the train slowed in each town, she woke long enough to look outside the window, searching for the sign that announced which town the train would stop in next. After briefly reviewing those who departed, or the few who boarded, she settled her head back and resumed her sleep. Deep sleep eluded her even when she laid and curled up on the seat.

At sunrise the train slowed for its arrival in Berlin. She saw through the window that the city had been damaged heavily since she had left. Buildings near the station lay in ruins. Only a handful had escaped the carnage. From her vantage point, most of the city seemed the same, some buildings stood; those in the industrial sectors had sustained the worst from the bombing.

Only three passengers occupied the seats when she stood, lugged the suitcase down from the carrier and made her way up the aisle.

When she stepped down onto the gravel by the rails, the city smelled different. The stench of smoke and sulfur hung heavy. The sky was overcast with unnatural looming clouds. Barely a half-dozen people stepped from the train. All of them moved in the same direction toward the rear of the train and uphill to the nearest street. Most of them, like her, surveyed the damaged buildings and deep holes in the dirt street.

She recognized the irony in the city. Berlin had risen from poverty after the Great War, confident in her European seat. Just months ago this had been a leading cultural center, beautiful and fresh. Now, the metropolis gasps to stave off the death throes.

Marianne carried the heavy suitcase uphill and around debris piles from buildings and torn streets. She made her way to the apartment building that she had fled. She stopped in the street out front to look up the long dark brick walls that still remain little worse for wear. She picked her way through the rubble and entered. The halls are dark and quiet. She unbuttons her coat before stepping up the staircase.

During daylight hours and for some time after, the dark hallways had always resounded with footsteps and voices. The air is so still now that dust motes hover undisturbed in light shafts piercing shadowy hallways.

She reached the half-opened doorway to the apartment where she had lived just days ago. She paused a moment before slowly pushing the door aside. The home was now a shambles from the air raid bombings.

With some effort she closed the front door and latched the lock. The apartment should bring fond memories however she had lived here for such a short time that she couldn't recall them.

Marianne hauled the suitcase to her bedroom and laid it open on the bed. She stripped off her clothes and then showered in the bathroom to wash away the dust from the train trip. After toweling off, she returned to the bedroom, chose a comfortable but flattering dress and high-heeled shoes. She packed the recently worn clothing inside, and laid out a pair of more comfortable shoes on top, just in case. After dressing and fixing her hair in the bathroom mirror, she closed the suitcase and lifted it from the bed. She made her way down the hallway, across the living room, and then stepped outside and into the hallway. She paused to listen to the silence.

A few doors down she knocked on the door to room three-seventeen and again listened for movement from inside. She knocked again before turning the doorknob. The door swung slowly open and she called, "Frau Schultz?"

Marianne stepped inside and called out, "Hallo?" The apartment is empty. No furniture or drapes, no lamps or even the small kitchen table that she remembered. The cupboard doors have been left open exposing bare shelves. She walked the short hallway, inspecting each bedroom and the bathroom to find the same.

When leaving, she carefully closed the door behind her. With her hands braced against the wooden railing, she looked up through the space in the hallways that reaches to the ceiling of the eight-floor building. "Hallo?" she called more loudly this time.

Convinced that everyone who had lived here is now gone, she made her way downstairs, lifted the suitcase and returned to the rubble filled street. After choosing a direction, she walked toward the center of Berlin. If any life worth knowing about is still in Berlin, she expected to find it in the city center.

After a particularly decimated row of buildings, she approached a tall apartment complex that remained largely intact. Several windows are open and curtains flutter from inside. A small group of people outside appear to have gathered for no particular reason. She passed unnoticed.

Occasional cars and trucks drive by on the street. After walking for two hours, she set the suitcase beside a bench and sat. She pulled off each shoe and rubbed the soles of her feet.

Over what little noise the street offered, the sound of several vehicle engines grew louder from the direction she had come. A block and a half away, a military staff car turned the corner and steered toward her, followed by truck after truck and more jeeps. Pairs of uniformed military troops ride in the staff cars, the rear of the trucks are filled with soldiers.

Marianne stood and ran her hands over her dress to smooth the wrinkles before stepping into the street. As the first staff car drew near she raised a hand, signaling the driver to stop. A German officer, judging by his uniform, in the passenger's seat motioned toward her and said something to the driver. The staff car pulled over in front of her.

The officer tipped his hat, "Guten Morgan, Fraulein."

Marianne smiled and locked her eyes on the officer. "Guten Morgan, Colonel. Might you be inclined to give a girl a lift to the center of the city? I've walked an awfully long way and I must be downtown by this afternoon."

"Why would you want to go downtown?" The Colonel asked. "You'll be much safer here, on the outskirts."

"Colonel..." she leaned forward and focused on his eyes, "do I look like a woman who hides in safety?"

The Colonel eyed her up and down, even leaning a bit to examine her high-heeled shoes. "Very well, get in."

The officer stepped from the staff car, lifted the suitcase into the back compartment and then offered his hand to help her into the backseat. Once she was seated the officer slid into the seat beside her. The engine growled, the driver shifted gears and resumed the drive. The trucks and jeeps followed behind them.

Marianne considered the Colonel; an attractive man, short cut graying hair, a handsome, clean-shaven face. The uniform nametag identified him as Colonel Gerste. Though considerably older than herself, he appeared fit. His stern eyes tell that he is not a man to be trifled with. When he boldly laid his left hand on her thigh she noticed the gold wedding band on his ring finger. She knew that a lonely soldier away from home can be a tricky undertaking. She also knew that every man finds his weakness in an attractive woman.

"So, Fraulein..." the colonel asked, plying her to offer a last name.

"Krankemann, Marianne Krankemann." She smiled.

"Who is it that commands your time downtown this evening?"

Marianne delicately removed the officer's hand from her thigh and answered, "Never a who, Colonel, a what. My apartment building has been damaged from the bombing and I'm without a home. I've lost everything. I hope that I might find work downtown, some task to earn money and eventually find a place to live."

"And what kind of work can you do?"

"Oh Colonel," Marianne said in her most seductive voice. "I have many talents. I'm an accomplished secretary, I type better than average. When I was a bit younger, I spent much time in the streets. A person educated in the streets could benefit your war efforts, you know."

"And how would that be?"

"Well," she leaned back against the door focused fully on him, "I've learned that truth is found in the streets. Street people know the heartbeat of the world around them without judgment. They know what is and what isn't, without the influence of bureaucrats. Yes, I could be of great help to you, for the right salary."

The Colonel laughed, "You are bold, Fraulein." He again laid his hand on her thigh. "I may have something to fit with your talents. I know of a quiet place with the best German steaks and an abundance of wine. Why don't we have dinner tonight to discuss it?"

She shook her head, "Dinner, no. I wouldn't feel right about lavish dining until I've at least found a place to sleep tonight; perhaps another time."

He waved his free hand, "A minor inconvenience. I believe you'll find my quarters in the city more than comfortable for a night or two, at least until you find something more suitable."

Again Marianne tactfully removed his hand to lay it aside. "Colonel, I can't help but notice your ring. Will we be staying with your wife?"

The officer's embarrassment was apparent in his blushing cheeks. "No, my wife lives down south in Stuttgart."

"I apologize if I've offended you, Colonel. I'm sure you have only the best intentions. I appreciate any assistance you might provide, and I'm certain we would work well together should you offer suitable work to match my skills. If I locate lodging for the night, how will I find you?"

The colonel pulled a slip of paper and a pencil from his breast pocket and began to write. "Do you know the city building downtown?"

She nodded, "Yes, I've been there many times."

"I've established a temporary command in the east wing. You'll find me there until six o'clock or so. After that," he offered the slip of paper, "You'll find me in my flat around eight, after dinner."

Marianne turned over the paper to read an address on the opposite side.

"Herr Stolinger operates a small apartment building east of the capitol building. Look in on him; tell him that I sent you. The living quarters are quaint and perhaps not up to your standards, but they may suit you temporarily." (Marianne occupied the apartment until 1945 when she rented another apartment in the city for some unknown reason.)

The staff car led the convoy around a corner and onto the main street before parking in front of the city building that the colonel had mentioned.

Marianne dropped the paper slip into her purse. "Thank you, Colonel. You are most kind."

The colonel patted the jeep driver's shoulder, "Kurt, drive Fraulein Krankemann anywhere in the city she chooses. Return immediately."

"Yes, Colonel," the driver answered.

Colonel Gerste stepped out and onto the sidewalk. He tipped his hat, "Fraulein, I trust we will meet again. It has been a pleasure."

"Thank you again, Colonel. You've been very generous. I hope to repay you one day."

The officer smiled thoughtfully and said nothing before turning and walking away.

As the driver pulled away, he asked, "Where to, Fraulein?"

Marianne handed the paper slip from the Colonel over the seat, "This address, please?"

The driver read the address and passed the slip back to her.

After dropping Marianne off at the address that Colonel Gerste had provided, she soon located Herr Stolinger, the owner. The Colonel had not overstated the simplicity of the small apartments, but Marianne figured a short term lease would benefit her until she could make other arrangements. Within the hour she had rented a frugally furnished apartment. She walked a short distance to the local market to purchase staples, then returned to bathe and put on her finest dress, which she considered considerably plain compared to the clothing and furs she had worn in the past. Since the return walk to the city building and Colonel Gerste's office was short, she left the new apartment at 5:30 P.M. Upon arriving at the city building, she asked the first officer that she met in the hallway to direct her to Colonel Gerste's office, which he kindly did.

Colonel Gerste stood from behind a desk when she entered. "Fraulein, I didn't expect to see you so soon!"

"Thank you, Colonel. I met with Herr Stolinger and have made arrangements to stay, at least for now. If the dinner invitation stands I wish to join you."

"Splendid! If you'll wait in the hall, I'll wrap up a few details and join you momentarily."

Marianne cocked an eyebrow and smiled, "Very well, don't keep me waiting long. I get restless, you know."

The colonel rested his hand against the small of her back and escorted her to the door with his apologies. Just as she stepped

43

outside, he said, "I'm pleased that you've decided to join me. I believe I have an interesting proposal for you. I'll be along in a few minutes."

## Chapter 5

Colonel Gerste smelled of fresh cologne when he left his office to join Marianne in the hallway of the city building. His uniform was crisp. This wasn't the uniform he had worn all day, she suspected, but one he held in reserve.

Again he placed his hand against the small of her back and escorted her from the building. Outside, Kurt waited in the same staff car that had brought them earlier. The drive to the steakhouse restaurant was short, giving her little time to press Colonel Gerste about the interesting proposal.

Despite the destruction to the city that Marianne had noticed, people must still provide for life's necessities. Those Berliners who had chosen to remain continued to work each day. Factories, of course, were crucial to the war effort, as were businesses that supported the military as well as the surviving citizens. Hospital staff though lean, were dedicated to caring for the sick and injured. So long as an establishment's building hadn't sustained heavy damage, business continued as usual. Grocery stores stocked and sold staples. Jewelers, law firms, furniture stores and street-side markets operated despite the looming danger.

*What drove people to remain through such destruction? Had they become so attached to their homeland that even the threat of death couldn't drive them away?* These thoughts ran through Marianne's mind while the colonel chatted away beside her.

Kurt slowed the staff car and parked along the walkway curb. The colonel stepped out and held the door for Marianne. The street was lined with cars and trucks as one might find on any other day before the bombing. She imagined that those vehicles that had been damaged had been removed to another part of the city.

Colonel Gerste opened the door of a windowed brick building and Marianne stepped inside ahead of him. The lights were low. A number of tables filled the front dining area of which more than half were occupied. A hallway ran toward the rear of the building. The atmosphere displayed a comfortable elegance that intrigued Marianne.

A young man dressed in black pants and a crisp white shirt approached from the hallway. He smiled when he spied the colonel. "Good evening, Colonel. A table for two this evening?" He gathered menus from a desk near the door.

"Yes, Fritz, just the two of us," the colonel replied.

"Right this way, please." Fritz motioned to Marianne before leading the couple through the hallway and into a private dining room off to the right. The lights were even dimmer in this room. Lone lit candles centered each of six tables dressed with fine, white table cloths, cloth napkins, crystal goblets and bone china place settings. From a center table Fritz collected two of the four place settings expertly in his arms. "The usual red-wine tonight, Colonel?"

Colonel Gerste slid back a chair and Marianne sat. "Excellent, yes," he said before Fritz departed. The colonel lifted a menu and handed it to her. "Fraulein, might I suggest the filet mignon? It's excellent here."

Marianne opened the menu and reviewed the selections briefly. "A filet it is," she said, closing the menu. "With a salad, please. I do so enjoy a good salad."

Fritz returned to pour the wine then took their order of two filet mignons, a salad, and a baked potato for the colonel. When Fritz again left the room, the colonel raised his wine glass toward Marianne.

"A toast, to our business venture," he offered with a hint of a smile.

Marianne raised her glass to touch his with a soft ringing tone. She sipped before setting the goblet back on the table. "Ah, you're proposal," she said. "What do you have in mind?"

The colonel sipped wine before setting the glass down in front of him. "As a rule, I don't discuss business over dinner, however, given your eagerness and time constraints, I'll make an exception."

He leaned forward placing his elbows on the table and intertwined his fingers supporting his chin. "You mentioned that you know the ways of the street. I require a courier with such skills to travel north and cross the front lines. Your duties may take you various places to obtain mercury, which is essential to the war effort.

"All you need do is to pick up small packages from my contacts, and transport them undetected back to Berlin."

Marianne studied his face and lowered her eyes. She raised the goblet and sipped. "And why don't your contacts just bring them across?"

Colonel Gerste shook his head slowly. "Too dangerous. These are highly sensitive materials. They would be instantly recognized and shot no matter how good their disguise. The Russians would never suspect a woman such as you."

"Well, I can't say I favor being shot, Colonel."

His smile widened as he again shook his head. "If you are caught, the Russians will never shoot a civilian woman. Only the soldiers suffer such a fate. No, at worst they may detain you for a short while."

The couple sat quietly when Fritz returned with their dinner plates and refilled their wine glasses before again leaving them alone.

"I trust that such risk will be rewarded handsomely?" Marianne finally asked.

Colonel Gerste sliced into the filet mignon and then forked a morsel into his mouth. While he chews, he nods and assures her, "Suitable payment will be rewarded upon delivery of each shipment. No salary. However, I am able to arrange a small advance for living quarters nearer the front lines."

He motioned with his fork toward her plate. "All of this talk ruins a splendid meal. Eat up, think it over. Come by my office in the morning and give me your answer." He raised his goblet toward her, "Long live the Führer."

Marianne simply lifted her glass and responded in kind.

Over the remaining time at dinner, the colonel asked after her past, her upbringing and her daughter, Christel. He showed slight concern over her staying on the farm and seemed intent with her story of living on the street and her paltry upbringing. Marianne omitted most details, unwilling to reveal too much of her life to a man that she barely knew. This she had also learned on the streets.

After finishing dinner they finished the remaining wine while talking until well past eight o'clock when Kurt appeared at the dining room doorway. Without acknowledging the driver, Colonel Gerste stood and escorted Marianne from the room.

The following morning and after a difficult night infrequent with sleep, Marianne made her way to the city building and Colonel

Gerste's office. The colonel stood from behind his desk and greeted her with a smile. "Come in, Fraulein! It's good to see such a beautiful face this early."

"Thank you, Colonel," she said while crossing the room. She followed his direction and sat in a chair across from him. When she sat he returned to his chair and asked, "I trust you've brought me good news?"

Marianne adjusted her position in her seat and tugged at the hem of her skirt. "Yes, I believe so. I'd like to give this a try and see if it fits. I believe I'll be a fine courier for the effort."

Colonel Goeste's face beamed. He loudly clasped his hands in front of him and stood. "Very, very good. You've made a wise decision."

"Yes, well, I thought I had made some wise decisions in the past that weren't so wise after all. This is a trial basis, no promises."

"Understood." The colonel rounded the desk when she stood. He lifted a manila folder from the desk and handed it to her. "Inside you will find the names of your contacts and your first station in Kaunas. You'll board the train this afternoon to Gdansk. In the morning, you'll catch an early train east to cross over the Eastern Front. In the north, the trains will not be inspected as thoroughly."

Colonel Gerste escorted her from the office and eventually out of the building while providing instructions.

"I'll arrange with Herr Stolinger to keep your room for your return to Berlin. You may be reassigned often in the north as the Front recedes."

As they stepped onto the walk, she spied Kurt waiting in the staff car. Colonel Gerste opened the door for her. When she was safely inside, he leaned in and kissed her cheek. "Travel safe. I have utmost confidence in you.

"Kurt, drive the Fraulein home." He directed his attention to her. "I'll send Kurt by at two-thirty to drive you to the station."

"Thank you, Colonel," she said while laying the packet on the seat beside her.

The Colonel turned abruptly and returned inside of the city building. Kurt started the staff car and pulled from the curb.

Kurt never spoke until he steered the staff car next to the walkway at Marianne's newly rented apartment. He stepped from the vehicle and opened the door for her, then said, "I suggest you rest. You may have a long few days ahead of you."

Marianne took his hand and stepped out, "Thank you, Kurt. You are most kind."

While she walked to her apartment, she didn't turn when the car engine started up and drove away. She held the manila envelope close to her stomach sensing how valuable the contents might be.

When inside, she locked and bolted the door then sat at the kitchen table. She carefully tore open the packet and slid the contents onto the table. She briefly read a sheet of paper that simply contained a name: Herr Konrad Fleischer, with an address. Below the name was an address in Kaunas, Lithuania. She opened a brown envelope next, the only other item inside the folder. Inside she found a small stack of German Deutsche Marks; enough for travel and to find living quarters when she reached her destination. *Yes,* she thought, *the colonel is most generous.*

Now the realization of her good fortune began to take hold. She had found work, enough money to tide her over for a time, and had a plan for the future. But what of a future that hinges solely on war? And what of the risk such an occupation brings? Was this a blessing, or her possible undoing?

For most of her life, Germany had been at war with someone, it seemed. She knew nothing of war, only what she had read in the newspapers or had heard on radio broadcasts. Everyone, it seemed, knew more about war than she did. And now she is destined to dance at the heart of it.

She pondered her situation while packing her meager belongings, and while she prepared lunch in the kitchen. The thought haunted her while eating. Despite the risk, she knew that desperate times called for big risk. With big risk came great reward or tragic failure. In reflecting back to a time when she had left home as a young girl, which seemed now so very long ago, she was confident that she had always faced adversity with a stout heart. This heart and good sense would see her through this as well.

She imagined details of bringing the packages across the front lines on the train, or in a car perhaps. At checkpoints, any man would be suspect, particularly young to middle-aged men. Women would be overlooked unless the soldiers are given to suspect otherwise. Even a male traveling companion might subject her to close scrutiny. She committed to always travel alone.

She lifted the paper and studied the name of Herr Konrad Fleischer, which had likely been scrawled in Colonel Gerste's own handwriting. The penmanship was firm and direct, containing no extraneous tails in the letters but was crisp and to the point, just as the colonel had been. *Yes,* she thought, *maybe Herr Fleischer can teach her more of smuggling.*

Marianne finished her lunch and dropped the remains in a wastebasket, then emptied it outside in the trash. She spent the early afternoon cleaning the apartment. She certainly hadn't lived here long enough to make much of a mess, but the task occupied her thoughts and tidiness had always been her nature. *Tidiness too,* she thought, *my behavior and appearance must be tidy and beyond suspicion.*

When the apartment was clean to her liking, she settled into the bath. After bathing, she changed into comfortable clothing suitable for a long train ride. When finished, she closed the suitcase and carried it to the front room.

She had just set the brown suitcase beside the door when through the window she saw Kurt slow the staff car outside. She gathered a light jacket and the envelope from the table. She paused to look around the small apartment, hoping to return soon. Then, she took a deep breath, lifted the suitcase and opened the front door.

Kurt met her halfway from the street and relieved her of the suitcase.

"You're right on time," she said.

"Yes, Fraulein, I try to be."

Kurt loaded the suitcase into the rear seat of the car and then held the door open for her until she slipped into the seat.

During the drive to the train station, she attempted small talk with Kurt to calm her nerves. The young man was quiet and seemed confident in his role as a soldier. Eventually he admitted that he hailed from a small town south of Strasburg and she wondered if he had joined the service, or if he had been recruited, a loose term for 'drafted'. She didn't ask. He said that he had played soccer through Gymnasium, the German equivalent to our high schools. Judging from his pride about the sport, she imagined that he had been quite good. His mother and father still lived at home. His father was a dairy farmer; his mother a baker who sold fresh bread and rolls from the farm.

When they pulled into the train yard, Marianne thought the yard was quite deserted compared to their previous escape from Berlin. Most people moving toward the train were soldiers with only a handful of civilians. Unlike the previous train that contained mostly passenger cars with a few freight cars, this train pulled only three passenger cars. The remaining were flatbed cars loaded with military personnel carriers, tanks and trucks. If she had underestimated her journey earlier, now she saw that she would ride into the heart of war.

On board the train Marianne found a vacant seat at the rear of the car. She stowed her lone suitcase in the overhead compartment, dusted off the worn seat upholstery with a handkerchief and sat.

She settled in to watch other passengers board; military men mostly. Two burly men with large duffle bags laughed and joked as they stored their gear; new recruits, she speculated, those who haven't yet seen the blood and death that battle offers so freely.

A young man and woman made their way down the aisle with two small children in their arms. The boy, about three-years-old, stared wide-eyed at nothing and everything. The younger girl slept in her mother's arms. Marianne suspected the girl was barely two-years-old; no longer a baby and still wrapped safely in the purity of her mother's love.

When the family finally sat after storing their worldly possessions, the boy stood on the seat and faced the rear of the train. His eyes locked on her, uncertain whether to smile. Perhaps she gave him too much credit but he studied her as though he suspected her secret. Where was she going? He must wonder. Why does she ride alone? Or perhaps her platinum hair is an enigma as children were so often enamored with her looks.

Passengers continued to filter in. Farmers, businessmen, lonely older men and women; all found seats until the last few were relegated to stand. An older gentleman who smelled of a farm sat beside her. His face was rugged and aged with soft gray beard stubble. The skin of his hands and his fingernails were soiled with dirt that couldn't be scrubbed away. She sensed a sadness from him that was likely the same, causing her to wonder if he had lost everything to the war, as she had. Despite the worn and tattered overcoat, she struck him as a hard-working and gentle man.

After what seemed like an eternity the hiss of the steam from the engine boilers began to louden. The wheels groaned and the train moved forward. The boy ahead finally settled into his seat. Within minutes the scenery out the window changed from ravaged Berlin streets to serene countryside. Green fields belied the tragedy that had befallen Germany. The rolling hills were alive with crops; corn, grain, vegetables, the essence of life. A small stream lined with young elm trees meandered through the valley.

The train stopped only briefly in town after town. Departing passengers were replaced by more soldiers, and small town transients traveling to imagined destinations.

Marianne stared aimlessly out the window at the particularly beautiful sunset. Again her mind wandered to earlier days on the streets where she had learned to be self-reliant and had gained no small amount of stubbornness. It seemed that she had spent more of her life without a home than with one.

She missed her daughter, but did she really? At least she knew that Christel was safe on the farm in Vilsbiburg. Now, she committed herself to make money to pay Herr Ackermann for Christel's upkeep.

She found the constant and tedious upheaval that was her life an enticement that had become rooted in her soul. Maybe this journey would finally rid her of the restlessness that held her. Perhaps this time she would find stability and a man who would love her for who she is. She could only hope that these rusted iron railroad tracks led to her destiny.

## Chapter 6

Before the harvest is over I decide that cutting wheat is lots of hot work. Not only did we harvest Herr Ackermann's wheat, but while the wheat dried in the field, we went to neighbors' farms and cut down their wheat too! I didn't have to pull water at every farm, only some of them. Sometimes I took food to the fields for the men, and sometimes I helped cook dinner. Romy always helps me learn things like cutting up vegetables. I like that but not the onions, onions make my eyes wet.

We eat so much food and we work so hard. Romy says farm people must work hard or they won't have a home to live in.

Mama came to the Ackermanns' when I was at the Bergman farm to harvest. After being away for so long, it was now mid-1944 and the war was not going well for Germany. When she found out we weren't at the farm, she and the other driver lady drove from farm to farm to find me. I was so excited to see her but sad that she hadn't found a home to take me to yet. She brought me clothes to wear for school though and she stayed for the dinner after we got done cutting wheat. I introduced her to Patch and she petted him while telling me that she had found work very far away and hoped to have enough money for a home soon. Around sunset she left to get on the train.

It has taken the whole two weeks from when we started harvesting until when school starts this morning to get all the wheat done.

Romy, Sabine and I gather the eggs this morning after letting the cows out of the Scheune. Frau Ackermann is mixing some things to make biscuits when we come back inside.

"Mama?" Romy asks. "Would you like help with the biscuits? I'm sure Christel and Sabine would love to help."

Frau Ackermann's eyes twinkle sometimes when she smiles. This is one of those times. "Sure," she says.

She lays out two bowls for Sabine and me. Romy helps us pour a little flour in each bowl and as I try to help, I spill some on the counter. Romy laughs and dips her finger in the flour, then taps the tip of my nose. This makes Sabine laugh but she wants a dot on her nose too, so Romy taps flour on her nose too.

I pinch a bit of flour between my fingers and put it on my tongue. It tastes like dust. Sabine tastes some then scrunches her nose and spits to get the flour off of her tongue.

Romy laughs and comes with a towel to wipe Sabine's tongue. "You goose," she says. "We don't eat raw flour, only when it's cooked."

I wonder how Romy's long, dark curly hair always falls in such perfect curls over her shoulders. I've helped her brush it to tame the curls and she usually brushes my hair before we go to sleep. By morning though, the brushing wears off and she has to do it again. Sometimes at night she sings a lullaby while we brush and I like those nights.

I pad the tips of my fingers into the flour bowl, then rap Romy right on her nose. Her eyes get really big and she looks at me serious, but I know she's not really mad. Romy never gets mad at anyone, that's just how she is.

She slaps both hands down in the flour and then puts her hands against my cheeks. When she pulls her hands away, she and Sabine laugh. I must look really funny.

"Oh, Romy..." Frau Ackermann scowls in a low voice. "Don't do such things to little girls." Then she comes and wipes the flour from my face with a towel. I dot her forehead with little flour spots.

I have never heard Frau Ackermann laugh before now. I like her laugh and know she has forgotten to worry about Viktor gone to war. We don't talk about that much but I know she worries about him because that's what Mama's do.

After breakfast we leave the house and Romy takes me by the hand. I'm glad Romy goes to school with us today. I'd be so scared to start school without her.

To get to school we walk all the way across the wheat field and into the forest. Patch walks with us until we get to the edge of the trees then Romy tells him to go back home.

I have seen forests from a long ways but I've never gone in one before. Forests have lots of trees and in some places it's dark because the sun can't get to the ground. In the dark places the air is colder. Forests smell so good! I smell flowers and trees and even can smell the streams before we cross them on a wide path that Romy says will take us to school. She has walked through this one a lot and I'm glad because other paths go off from this one and I know we would get lost if she wasn't with us.

All of us kids stay very quiet walking through the trees. We see squirrels and birds, rabbits and seven deer. Romy warns us to stay together because we can get lost real easy.

Sabine holds Romy's hand too. Letta and Gretchen walk right behind us. Gretchen is new, she just came yesterday. Gretchen has known the Ackermanns for a very long time. Her mom and dad had to go away so she lives with us now. She is the same age as Letta and they are together a lot. Dieter and Franz follow in the back to keep an eye on everyone so we don't get lost.

In the darkest places of the woods we walk very fast, or run to get through to the sunlight. This is a scary forest and I don't know what other kinds of animals might live in here. Wolves maybe and maybe even some scary men, I don't know. Even Romy doesn't like it much.

When we leave the forest we cross a ditch and come up to a dirt road. We follow the road past some fields and eventually arrive at the school.

The school is painted red and has only one door and some windows. It's not even as big as Romy's house. The grass around the school is tall but not as tall as the wheat before we cut it. Yellow and blue flowers grow in the grass. Romy stops so Sabine and I can smell the flowers and we each pick only one. Romy puts the flowers in our hair to celebrate our first day of school.

Inside the school has only one room and is smaller than it looks from the outside. A lady sits behind a big desk in the front and a chalk board takes up almost the whole wall behind her. Other kids are already in the room and they sit at desks. We sit in empty desks along the wall. Pretty soon a few other kids come in and sit down and only two desks are left empty.

Romy is the oldest in the room except for the lady behind the desk. Some kids are a little older than me and some are much older.

The lady at the desk stands up, looks at all of the kids and says, "Guten Morgan, everyone. So many new faces today.

"I am Frau Kaestner. I live just up the road a little ways. Now, I'd like you all to tell me your names, and how old you are." She points to Franz in the front corner. "Would you begin, junger Mann?"

Franz's face is real red when he stands up and says, "My name is Franz Gottlieb and I'm fourteen." He sits down fast. Everyone takes their turn and stands up, says their name and tells how old they are.

When my turn comes, I tell her that my name is Christel Krankemann, and I am five years old.

The other kids are very quiet and I stay quiet too. We aren't supposed to talk unless we talk to the teacher. We learn some about numbers and she tells us a story about how important it is to do well in school. Finally Frau Kaestner says it's time for recess and we all go outside for a little bit. We drink water from a pump then Sabine and I walk with Romy through the tall grass and look at all the flowers.

"How do you like school?" Romy asks.

Sabine shrugs and I answer, "It's hard to sit for so long. I would rather play or be at the farm with Patch."

"Yeah, me too," Sabine agrees with me.

"School is very important," Romy says. "Everyone goes to school so they can be smart. You'll find some things you like to learn, and others won't be as much fun, but it's all important. One day you will want to find work, and a good education helps you find jobs that you like and pay lots of money."

"You will be out of school soon, Romy," Sabine says. "What kind of job will you have?"

"I'd like to be an actress."

I ask, "What's an actress?"

Romy sits on the grass. She tilts her head back to look at the sky and her curls touch the grass. "Have you ever seen a movie?"

We shake our heads.

"Or a play?"

Again we shake our heads.

"Oh, we must see a movie and a play sometime. Men are called actors, and the women are actresses. They play a pretend game that tells stories."

Sabine asks, "What kind of stories?"

Romy lies back on the grass and we sit next to her. "All kinds of stories; love stories, sad stories, happy stories and some with great adventures."

"You'll be a good actress," I say. "You tell good stories."

"In some plays the actors even sing," she says. "Maybe I'll have a singing part too."

I know that Romy will be a good actress then because she sings like an angel.

"Come take your seats!" Frau Kaestner calls from the school porch.

Romy stands and takes our hands. We walk inside with the other kids and sit at the same desks we had before.

Since the kids in class are all different ages, sometimes the teacher says things that we little kids don't have to listen to. Other times, she teaches us things that the older ones already know, so they usually read from big books or write on papers. I want to learn to write because it looks like fun. I don't have to wait long to learn because after lunch Frau Kaestner teaches us to write the alphabet. All of the letters are on the board and we copy them onto paper. This is fun but very hard trying to make the letters look the same. It's like drawing a picture but you have to draw exactly what the letter looks like. If you don't, only you can read what you wrote and this is not good. Romy helps Sabine and me. It takes us a long time to write all twenty-six letters and when I finish I don't think writing is much fun anymore.

We have one more recess and I'm glad because my fingers are very tired from holding that pencil. Dieter and Franz play tag with the other kids from the school. They always make friends fast and I wish that I could do that too. Letta and Gretchen sit across the lawn at the edge by the trees and watch the kids, probably deciding which boy is the cutest. That's what they always do. I don't think boys are cute. Baby pigs are cute; boys are trouble. Except for Viktor; Viktor is the cutest boy I know and I miss him.

I think of Viktor often through the school year. I remember our rides across the property to watch the sunset. The Ackermanns talk about him a lot and especially Romy. I know she loves him. Herr and Frau Ackermann talk about the war sometimes but always stop when a kid comes into the room. They like to talk to us about Viktor though and for the first time I wish that I had a brother.

My favorite thing in school is coloring. I draw pictures of the farm, the trees, sometimes leaves or bushes. I've never had crayons before, well, maybe once when I was too little to remember. Romy always pretends to like my drawings and Sabine's too, even if I draw better than Sabine.

Each afternoon when we come out of the forest and into the Ackermann's field, Patch is already waiting to walk home with us. Some days we try to walk the last part really quiet so he won't know we are coming, but he's always there. That dog has good hearing.

In the late fall, Herr Ackermann picks out two cows and two pigs then loads them in a big truck and takes them off to the slaughterhouse. Romy says when he drops the animals off at the slaughterhouse; they give him lots of meat to bring home. Something must have happened though because he didn't go back to town for three days to pick up the meat. And boy what a lot of meat! The meat is cold and hard and we carry it all down into a root cellar where Herr Ackermann puts in big blocks of ice to keep the meat cold. Winter is cold in Germany and when it gets coldest, Herr Ackermann doesn't have to put more ice in the cellar.

Another six months has passed and Mutti, (Mama) appears to bring warm winter clothes, a fluffy jacket and boots that keep me warm when we walk to school. I can slide on the ice with the boots and the cold doesn't bother my feet at all. Mama stayed two days this time and she often cooked with Frau Ackermann and me and Romy. It was fun to see her for so long. She tells me that she is working hard to find us a home and I believe her.

Mama says that all of my work on the farm, the good food and the exercise walking to school "suits" me. I'm not sure what that means but I feel stronger and bigger and I never get sick like some of the other kids.

After Mutti leaves I wonder where she is going or what she is doing all of the time that she is away. She never says anything and never talks about herself.

Franz and Dieter move away from the farm in the spring with their mama. Most of the kids leave but Gretchen, Sabine and I stay. We all like the farm and don't mind the work. We don't have anything to do but go to school and work and play.

Eight days after Franz and Dieter left the farm, we all return from school to find a shiny black car and an army truck parked in the driveway. I think it might be more children coming to live with us but Romy looks really sick when she hurries us to the house. She takes our school books and tells us to go check on the pigs, and to stay and play in the barn until she comes for us.

Although Romy doesn't say so, I'm afraid something is wrong and I don't know what. Sabine and I toss a little bit of grain to the pigs. We're not supposed to because they are only supposed to eat in the mornings, but I think they must get hungry in the afternoon too.

Sabine and I take Patch into the barn and we sit quietly to wait on the hay bales. We talk a little but we don't have much to say. We both worry about Romy's family.

"I hope we don't have to go away," Sabine says finally.

The thought of leaving the farm makes my tummy a little sick. "I hope so too," I tell her. I take her hand and hold it in my lap. "We'll be okay. Romy will take care of us."

It's a while before Romy returns to the barn. When she does, her eyes are red and swollen and I know she's been crying. Sabine and I run to her. Patch circles us barking while we hug her. Romy wipes her wet cheeks with both of her hands and then guides us back over to the hay bales where we sit.

"Why are they here?" I ask, not knowing exactly who I'm referring to.

Romy puts an arm around each of us and pulls us in close. "Some men from the war are here. They've brought Viktor home."

I'm excited to see Viktor but still don't understand why her eyes are so red. When people are happy they might cry a little, but not enough to make their eyes this red.

I ask, "Can we see him?"

Romy shakes her head and softly says, "No, Sprite. I'm sorry, you can't see him."

I'm not sure what to say, so I don't say anything.

She holds us tight for a moment before continuing. "Viktor died in the war. The men brought him back to be buried."

I don't believe what she says. Viktor can't die; he's much too big and strong. Even though I'm only five I know about death. Death comes to take old people away. Death doesn't come to take boys like Viktor.

Outside I hear men talking and then soon I hear the car and the truck drive away. Karl appears in the Scheune doorway. He blinks his eyes to adjust to the darkness and calls, "Romy?"

"I'm here, Karl." Romy says.

Karl looks over to the hay bales where we sit, and says, "Papa needs our help."

"I'll be along in a minute."

Karl turns and steps outside the door.

Romy's arms shake now as she holds us. "I need you two to be strong now," she says. "Crying is okay. We'll talk tonight before bed. For now, we have work to do."

She stands and we follow her from the barn. Outside, all of the children stand around a big wooden box that sits in the dirt place between the house and the Scheune. Herr Ackermann stands with his arm around Frau Ackermann and he looks very sad. Frau Ackermann has red eyes and wet cheeks like Romy. When we approach, Herr Ackermann says, "Everyone grab hold. Let's carry this to the barn."

I fit into a little corner beside Romy. I'm not sure what is in the box but it is very heavy. I do my best to keep up with the others and carry my share. Herr Ackermann says to carry it gently and we do. Inside the barn we hold the box while Karl moves some bales to make a table where we can set it down.

Frau and Herr Ackermann and Karl stay in the barn when Romy leads the rest of us to the house. We all sit in the kitchen while Romy and Ingrid pull items from the cupboard and the ice box to make sandwiches for dinner. Frau Ackermann comes in and helps before she's finished. We all eat quietly. Herr Ackermann won't join us because I hear him drive off on the tractor. I expect he has taken Karl with him because he doesn't come in to eat.

When we finish dinner, Romy says, "Children, let's all dress up tonight. Take fast turns in the bathroom. Wash your faces and brush your hair. We'll dress in our finest clothes. I'll help the little ones. Everyone meet back here when you're finished, okay?"

Ordinarily this would sound like a fun game to me, but Romy doesn't sound happy. This is a serious game, I'm sure.

It doesn't take long for Sabine and me to wash up and dress with Romy helping us. Sabine wears a pretty pink Sunday dress and I wear my best one. It's white and for church, but we have only gone to church once since I came to the farm.

We wait in Romy's room while she dresses and then sits on her stool and brushes her hair. Romy takes longer than usual to get ready, but not much longer.

When we return to the kitchen all of the children are there. Herr Ackermann and Karl haven't returned yet, and now Frau Ackermann is gone too.

"Come along," Romy says as she holds the door open for us. We all go outside and she leads us to Frau Ackermann's special part of the garden where she grows flowers. The air begins to cool. I can't see the sky behind the blanket of dirty clouds. Only a little bright glow tells me the sun is setting low over the hills. The sky sometimes gets like this before night.

"If you wish, you may pick just one flower," Romy tells us. "Pick the prettiest you can find."

Sabine and I walk carefully together through the garden away from the other children. I've helped Frau Ackermann pull weeds before so I know where the best flowers are. Finally I reach the patch I'm looking for and I help Sabine pick the most beautiful red flower. Then I pick a pink one that is just as nice.

When we all have a flower, Romy leads us out toward the drive where the cars come in. She stops and waits for the slower kids to catch up, then says, "We'll walk out to the edge of the trees where Papa and Mama are. On the way, please walk quiet. Think about Viktor and how much fun he always was. Think of his smile that we all enjoyed so much." Then we all start to walk through the field, following the path we take to school.

I wish Viktor was here. I want him to lead me on Bessie so we can watch the sunset. I imagine his smile and even hear him laugh. It's funny how our brain works that way sometimes.

When we get closer to the edge of the woods where the path to school leads, Romy leads us off to the right and I see the tractor first. Then, I see Herr and Frau Ackermann and Karl waiting for us.

Herr Ackermann looks old and tired. While he never seems very happy, he is always strong and steady while he works. Today his shoulders droop down. Maybe it's the light from the sun through the clouds that makes him look gray. Everything looks grayer than usual.

The tractor is parked off to the side with a wagon behind it. The big wooden box sits next to a deep hole that Herr Ackermann and Karl must have dug before we got here. Frau Ackermann has all of us kids gather around the box.

Frau Ackermann hands a bible to her husband and he opens it and reads some out loud for us. Then, he talks some about Viktor and asks God to take care of him. It's then that I realize that Viktor is inside the box.

Romy's eyes are wet and she wipes her cheeks with a handkerchief. Then, all of us kids lay our flowers on top of the box and say goodbye to Viktor. Some of the kids start to cry though I don't know why because they never knew Viktor like I did. Some of them came after Viktor had already gone to the war. I don't cry but my eyes are a little wet and my tummy hurts.

After we say goodbye, Romy leads the children back to the farm house. We walk quietly. Back at the farmhouse we all change into our nightclothes and get into bed before the sky is even dark. When the house is quiet, I hear Romy crying from her bedroom. I'm sad for her. Sabine breathes softly and I know she is asleep.

I gather up Baby Anna and Teddy then get out of my bed, something I never do after Romy tucks me in. We walk very quietly into the hall. I stand outside of her room and look inside. She sits on the bed dressed in her blue flowered nightgown. She looks up and sees us looking in. She quickly brushes over her eyes with her hands. "Can't you sleep, Sprite?"

I shake my head. Romy invites us in by patting the bed beside her. I cross the room and sit on the bed, unsure of what to say. She rubs my back and says, "It's been a long day. You should be tired."

I nod and lay Teddy on her lap. Romy's long lean fingers smooth the fur on Teddy's face. She brushes a tear with the back of her hand, and asks, "Would you guys like to sleep with me tonight?"

I nod again.

We stand from the bed and Romy pulls back the down comforter and sheets. Then, we climb into bed and she pulls the covers over us. I snuggle next to her with Baby Anna secure in my arms. I like how Romy smells like flowers. When she holds me I feel very special. Romy runs her fingers through my hair and soon my eyes get heavy.

I'm five years old now, it's near the end of 1945 and I have been at the farm for nearly two years.

## Chapter 7

Seven weeks had passed since Marianne's arrival in Kaunas, Lithuania. She found Kaunas to be a simple unassuming town despite being thrust back and forth between countries vying for world domination. The townsfolk were simple too, content in daily life when the war allowed them to be.

Marianne had formulated a plan before departing the train. She had committed to change her appearance not only for smuggling mercury, but in her daily life. It became important to her to remain anonymous, unseen, and nearly invisible. An attractive young woman such as she is would draw attention. An elderly woman, however, could pass through enemy lines above suspicion.

Upon the train's approach to Kaunas, Marianne had carried her lone suitcase to the restroom. In the cramped quarters she had changed into a rather plain flowered dress, an old sweater that she kept for chilly nights, and shoes that unfortunately were too fine to match the outfit. She bound her hair in a bun, and then set about transforming her face with makeup to appear older than her years. The process was simple really, as long as a person didn't scrutinize her closely. Marianne felt confident that in passing a person wouldn't be inclined to study her closely. Her goal was to appear elderly and ordinary. Who really allows their gaze to linger on an elderly woman while passing in the street?

To avoid further suspicion, Marianne carried her suitcase through the passenger car behind where she had traveled and then into the next. While walking she feigned a slight limp and lugged the suitcase as though it contained heavy bricks. She found a vacant seat in the center of the car and a middle-aged gentleman assisted her in lifting the luggage into the overhead compartment. Before sitting she patted his arm as she had often seen elderly women do.

The day after her arrival she had met Herr Konrad Fleischer, the man that Colonel Gerste had instructed her to contact. Herr Fleischer owned the only butcher shop in town and was the only person who knew the secret of her elderly appearance.

Each morning before Marianne left her humble apartment, she took great pains to recreate the face as she had on the train. She had purchased more clothing and a worn pair of shoes in a second hand shop to complete her disguise.

In the past, Marianne, as an attractive and curvaceous blonde had attracted attention from male admirers no matter where she went. As an old woman, Marianne could pass unnoticed by most people. The only exception seemed to be the Russian soldiers; a soldier's duty is to be nosy, she learned.

Each day she wandered the small town, alternating grocery shopping at various markets to avoid becoming familiar. She spoke little and then only when spoken to. She had carried mercury via train on six occasions and had been above suspicion. Deliveries of the precious metal paid well, better than the money she had earned at any job in the past.

Germany struggled in the war; the Allies were closing in from the west and the Russians approached from the east. Marianne's undercover work became hazardous. Mercury was never more vital to the war effort than it was now. Mercury is used in armament switches, relays and sensors, fuel and batteries and navigation equipment. How much of what she carried was actually for the war effort or for personal gain of those involved? She never spoke of this to anyone and maybe she never knew.

When she traveled, the soldiers were more attentive to young men and attractive women. At these times, she knew she had pulled off her plan to be invisible. Not once had she been questioned or searched; for this, she was grateful.

Divisions of Russian soldiers passed through Kaunas on their way to battle at the front. A few, however, were stationed to patrol the town. Those faces became familiar to her particularly in the center of town at the public water well that provided water to residents. One young soldier often watched over the well, getting to know the townsfolk, loitering and watching. This young man, she knew, could endanger her plans.

The Russian soldiers for the most part were friendly and amiable. Distanced from the front, they seemed to enjoy their tedious assignment of protecting the town of Kaunas which hadn't needed much protection, at least not in the weeks since her arrival. The uniformed men often traveled in groups of two, three, or four, laughing and joking with each other. When they traveled together, she noticed that they paid little attention to the old woman shuffling down the walk with her bucket in hand. However, the young soldier near the well always stood alone, watching.

The soldier was polite enough and often nodded when she passed. Occasionally he assisted her in drawing water, which brought him closer than she preferred. He said little, as did she. She found him attractive, handsome even, and stoic. If she hadn't needed to maintain the appearance of the old woman, she'd have much preferred to share a conversation with him and possibly dinner out and drinks. But, the world was what it was, and for now, she would continue to keep him at a distance.

Over the weeks since her arrival she had used the makeup sparingly. Still, her supply ran low. Each night when she washed the makeup off, she fretted. Each morning when she reapplied the disguise, the bottles emptied a little more. She had searched the stores to replenish her supply without success. Apparently in a small town the demand for cosmetics didn't warrant a shopkeeper's inventory as they had in Berlin.

Over the next several months, Marianne lived a clandestine life. She knew no one in town closely, not even Herr Fleischer. Konrad was a pleasant family man with a wife and three children. Through his daily work of butchering meat for the residents, Herr Fleischer intimately knew each of the townsfolk and their history. He knew a select few who could be trusted. He had even developed some rapport with the Russian soldiers since soldiers require meat like everyone else.

Despite the meager war economy, Konrad's butcher shop remained stocked with fresh chickens and ducks, turkey, rabbit, and of course red meats from cattle and even goats. Herr Fleischer's smokehouse out back of the shop belched daily while fresh made sausages and bacon absorbed rich smoke flavors. He had been particularly kind to Marianne in providing her ample supplies of fresh meat at little or no cost. It was his way, he said, of contributing to the war effort even beyond his smuggling contacts.

By now, Marianne's makeup supply was long gone. She did her best to use soil dampened with water to at least maintain a haggard appearance. By grinding graphite from writing pencils into fine powder, she effectively hid her natural beauty to remain unnoticed especially during the train journeys across to Germany.

The Russian soldier at the water well seemed to be the only person to notice Marianne's changed appearance. He frequently studied her more closely, often helping her draw water and looking directly into her face when he hadn't in the past. Then, one evening as she approached the well to draw water to wash her dinner dishes, a new face had replaced the familiar soldier. The new soldier stood tall and broad and took little interest in the townsfolk.

Over the next week, the watchful soldier failed to appear. Finally Marianne surmised that he must have shipped out. *Good riddance,* she thought, relieved because he had come too close and too often.

One cold November night in 1944 while riding the train with her suitcase laden with tubes of mercury, Russian soldiers stopped the train between Kaunas and the Russian battle lines. A troop of soldiers methodically inspected nearly every passenger and their luggage. Marianne slumped low in the seat and drew a scarf around her face. When three soldiers stopped and ordered her to stand, one soldier gently drew back her scarf to view her face. She recognized the soldier from the well even before he greeted her.

"Guten Abend, Fraulein." The soldier's steely gaze told her that he had recognized her.

"Guten Abend," she said firmly.

The soldier motioned with his head to the overhead luggage compartment. His two companions pulled down her suitcase and within seconds the men discovered the mercury.

The first soldier held his rifle to her chest and spoke in Russian. She surmised from his motions with the gun barrel that she was to turn and place her hands on the overhead compartment. She glared at him for a long moment before she complied. A second soldier searched her roughly for weapons. Then, the soldier from the well spoke in broken German, informing her that he was arresting her for treason. He placed the rifle barrel against her ribs and firmly directed her toward the train car door.

Marianne walked slowly to the exit. The other passengers glanced quickly when she passed as though afraid to draw attention from the soldiers and perhaps suffer the same fate.

Her skin felt clammy. Droplets of sweat beaded on her forehead. Her underarms were sticky and damp. She realized her breathing was shallow and her face was flushed with fear.

Thankfully the soldiers spoke little after that and she was convinced that once outside they would shoot her and the train could continue on its way. The months of hiding had now come to an end.

Once outside however, the soldiers didn't shoot her. Rather, they marched her to a waiting truck that contained three other men and one woman, all from the train, she suspected. Before the truck drove away she realized that the five of them were now war prisoners.

The truck drove down long, potholed roads for hours. They passed through towns and no one on the street paid them any mind. After a half-hour drive along a tree-lined dirt road, the truck eventually stopped at a large wooden and wired gate. Two soldiers opened the gate. The truck entered before the soldiers pulled the gate closed behind them.

Judging from the position of the setting sun, Marianne estimated the small prison camp lay some distance north of Kaunas. The camp was relatively small compared to the war camps that she had heard of. Some, the stories told, contained hundreds and even thousands of prisoners. This camp however, a temporary holding facility no doubt, couldn't house more than a few dozen people, she judged by the number of wooden shacks.

Immediately after their arrival, Marianne and four others joined ten other prisoners and were herded into a small room. There, they were ordered to strip and were searched without regard to gender. The soldiers then moved them outside where the prisoners were hosed down with fire hoses. The force of the water assaulted her skin. Fumes from the decontaminating chemicals burned her eyes and nose. Without being allowed to dry off, each person was issued ill fitting, drab clothing and worn boots that fit no better.

The soldiers separated the group into three and four people per group and led them to separate shacks. Inside of the shack, Marianne found eight rows of bunk beds each stacked three high. Most were occupied. She climbed into a vacant lower bunk, pulled a smelly wool blanket up around her head and attempted to sleep.

By sunrise sleep had eluded her. Two Russian guards rousted the prisoners from their bunks and marched them outside. Marianne was surprised to see more than a hundred and fifty prisoners form a line outside of the largest building in the compound. Before she fell in line, a young soldier pulled her from the milling group and escorted her to a doorway to the side of the building where the others entered. *This is it,* she thought. *This will be my last day on earth.*

The armed soldier directed her down a hallway and into a small room with an open door. Inside the room, a balding, iron-jawed Russian Officer sat behind a desk, leafing through papers. Her suitcase rested beside the desk.

When Marianne approached, the soldier pulled a chair from along the wall, placed his hand on her shoulder and forced her to sit. The man behind the desk looked up to the soldier and simply nodded. The soldier stepped back, held the rifle securely over his chest and blocked the doorway.

Despite the Russian uniform, the man behind the desk spoke fluent German, "You are a spy."

Marianne shook her head slowly, forcing a weak smile. "No, sir. A smuggler maybe, but not a spy."

The officer leaned back in the chair, placed both hands behind his head and studied her. "How long have you smuggled mercury?"

Marianne lowered her head and quietly answered, "Is that what that is? I had no idea."

"Surely, Fraulein, don't think me a foolish man." The officer stood to circle the desk and stand beside her. He fingered a lock of her hair. Her most recent disguise attempt had obviously failed. She'd been unable to achieve her aged appearance but she knew that she still looked ragged and tired. She *was* tired after not having slept since yesterday morning. Her hair was tangled and just short of ratted. Her face, hands, and neck were dirty and glistened with sweat. Her tattered clothing, designed to detract from her appearance, reeked. She hoped that her odor wouldn't offend the officer as it did her.

He said, "We've known for some time that mercury and other prohibited goods were making their way across. We had no idea how, until now."

She shook her head again, "With all due respect, sir. I was asked to carry this suitcase to Warschau for a friend. That's simply all I know."

"You're telling me that you haven't smuggled mercury for the Germans?"

"No sir, at least not knowingly." Marianne looked up, sincere with tired green eyes. "I'm a simple woman trying to earn money to live. I have no interest in your war."

"Then this person paid you to deliver the suitcase?"

"Yes sir, thirty Deutsche Marks; a paltry sum but enough to buy groceries for my daughter."

The officer stepped away and sat at his desk. He took up a pencil and laid a clean sheet of paper in front of him. "What is the name of the person who asked you to deliver the suitcase?"

"Herr Schmidt, Peter Schmidt," she said, knowing that the name was as common as rainfall during a German summer.

The officer wrote on the paper. "And you boarded the train in Kaunas?"

She nodded, "Yes, sir."

"And Peter Schmidt lives in Kaunas?"

"Yes."

"Who were you to deliver the luggage to?"

"That I don't know, I'm sorry."

The officer looked at her curiously.

"I was to leave the suitcase unattended below the clock tower in the Market Square at precisely noon today. I assume that whoever the case is intended for would pick it up."

The officer jotted notes on the paper, shook his head and said, "You give me little, Fraulein. I will find this Peter Schmidt, and if he verifies your story, we will arrest him and release you. I will most likely shoot him." His steely gray eyes focused on her. "If we cannot locate him, I will be forced to assume that you are the spy." He motioned to the soldier with his pencil.

The soldier stepped forward and lifted her suitcase. Marianne stood and turned without a word. The soldier escorted her from the office.

Although Marianne had faced difficult circumstances during her life on the streets, she was terrified when she left the office. In the past, her actions and decisions had determined her fate. Here, her life lay solely in the hands of the man behind the desk. Outside she eyed the tall barbed-wire fence surrounding the compound while the soldier accompanied her to the end of the dwindling line of prisoners entering a doorway. Three manned guard towers loomed at four corners of the compound, providing the guards with an unobstructed view of the fence-line and outer perimeter. Beyond the fence, thirty-yards of open field lay where the trees had been cut away. Even if she were to breach the fence, the guards would cut her down before she could make the distant tree line.

Last in line, she neared the door and detected the odor of food. The smell was unfamiliar and certainly wasn't meat or any fine fare. No matter, she hadn't eaten since having a sandwich at lunch before boarding the train and she welcomed nourishment.

The soldier set the suitcase beside her and left. When the line moved forward, Marianne lifted the suitcase, advancing it a few feet at a time before setting it down. She wondered what if any of her items the officer had left inside the suitcase. She dared not open the case here; it would have to wait until she returned to her bunk.

When she reached a table inside, a server slopped something resembling warm paste onto a metal tray, added a crust of bread and a tin cup filled with water. He thrust the tray toward her without a glance. Marianne carried the tray and made her way to an empty chair at a long table with other prisoners. All sat wordlessly eating the same paste as was on her tray. When finished, without acknowledging anyone around them, each prisoner filed from the room.

Marianne broke the crust of bread, sopped up the paste and bit into the mess. Bland and tasteless, old oatmeal she decided. While she ate, she studied the lifeless figures that left the room. Each of them looked dead inside. She saw no children; all were young to middle-aged adults. The lack of children seemed out of place to her, but she was grateful that innocent children were not imprisoned here, no matter the joy they might have brought to the others.

The prisoners were dirty and tired. It wasn't hard for her to distinguish those who had been here for a while from the new arrivals like herself. Those that had been here for some time were thin and drawn. Their skin was pallid and their eyes lacked the spark of life.

The skin of the new arrivals, despite their confused demeanor, at least retained the pinkish glow of the living. They seemed aware of those around them even if they didn't have the courage to speak.

The soldiers who made their way through the dining crowd looked like clones to her. Each was dressed in a sharp, clean uniform. Their haircuts were buzzed short, their faces freshly washed and even their fingernails were dirt free. These men had not been to the front line yet, she reasoned. Perhaps they were privileged men of Russian society whose family or friends had pulled strings to secure them relatively easy duty.

And the soldiers were handsome; all of them fit and toned. Even their jawlines were firm. No matter the color of their eyes, they sparkled with purpose.

One such soldier passed close by her table and barely glanced toward her, something that seemed unusual to her. She began to form a plan.

While she had crafted the old woman in Kaunas to go unnoticed, that charade no longer served her in a prison compound. Here, she must be noticed, noticed by the soldiers. Perhaps for special favors, extra portions at mealtime, maybe a chocolate bar and, god forbid, maybe the right soldier could procure makeup.

After leaving the mess hall, she found that sometime during the camp construction, the builders had drilled a water well smack in the middle of the compound. Just as in the town of Kaunas, camp residents were drawn to socialize around the rusted iron hand pump. Perhaps socializing was a strong word, residents more properly milled around, saying little, but gathered at the spot just the same.

Committed to her new cleanliness regimen, Marianne fashioned wash cloths by tearing a soft blouse that had once been her favorite. She stored the seven bits of cloth tucked safely beneath her bunk blankets as though they were hidden treasure.

Three times each day she knelt at the pump and wet a cloth, scrubbing her face, arms and legs. Eventually she rid herself of the months of ground in makeup and grit from the soil and graphite. Her skin returned to a healthy pinkish glow. No matter what slop she received in the mess hall, she ate every morsel. Undoubtedly the food, if it could be referred to as such, provided little nutritional value but, she reasoned, if she ate enough her body just might get what it needed to remain healthy.

Staying healthy in the compound might prove daunting. Prisoners were frail and sickly. Open sores were the norm and uncleanliness common. Although good hygiene must be essential to carry out her plan, she understood the view of the others; those who had abandoned hope. They could not see beyond the high wire fences. Most, she noticed, didn't look toward the fence or surrounding field to the cool shelter of the forest. They hadn't noticed the carefree clouds in the blue sky. No one else looked to the stars after dark and dreamed. No, they were resigned to a fate that is no fault of their own. Fate delivered through war conceived by men with false pride. Such reason lay beyond her world of survival, but nonetheless she understood it.

As she stood at the fence looking out after her morning bath, she saw hope in the trees. The trees had stood long before the destruction, and with a little help from God's hand, they would stand long after this camp had deteriorated.

She turned to look to the closest guard tower and the soldier who watched her. The man stood stoic on the tower deck with his rifle across his chest. His steely eyes took her in, and everything around her. He missed nothing, she imagined. If she were to conceal a small weapon beneath her baggy clothing, he would know.

She had seen him only occasionally at dinner in the mess. Around noon each day a soldier delivered his lunch by climbing the narrow ladder. She imagined that he had eaten breakfast before climbing to his post before dawn to relieve the night watch. The soldiers in the compound ate the same food as the prisoners, but she suspected they might bring in extra goodies during leave when they ventured into the nearest town, wherever that might be.

She raised a hand to wave and smiled. The soldier remained unmoving except for a slight nod of his head. *What does he think of me?* She wondered. *Is he married? Does he have children?* Although he was young, he looked old enough to have taken a wife, and perhaps fathered children. Did he wonder the same about her? *Unlikely*, she decided.

The call of a bird drew her attention back to the edge of the forest where a lone black crow sat atop a tree. She smiled.

## Chapter 8

For the next two weeks Marianne religiously continued her daily wash schedule. Conversations were difficult with the other prisoners as most of them seemed caught in a haze that she was unable to penetrate. The soldiers were even less approachable. Now and then she smiled and nodded to one or two in passing but received a minimal response. She wondered if they somehow felt remorse for imprisoning souls who were no more or less human than they were. If so, the distance they maintained was understandable. If one didn't look directly into the face of death, then perhaps one could avoid it.

The exception was one young soldier who sometimes smiled or even spoke to her when he saw her at the water well. He seemed to notice that she stood apart from the others.

He had once told her that his name was Theodor and his bright brown eyes glistened with life; a refreshing change from the lifelessness that she saw in the prisoners and the cold gray eyes of the other soldiers. Wisps of bright blonde hair peeked from beneath his army helmet. His shoulders were broad and square, and he stood at least a head taller than her.

One clear day as she stood at the fence watching the woods, Theodor approached to stand beside her. Concealed from the view of the tower watch guard, he slipped a large, fresh dinner roll into her coat pocket. Later that night she ate it quietly in her bunk while the others slept.

The weather over the compound had remained mostly pleasant. Marianne always enjoyed watching the changing clouds that loomed most days before sunset. When storms came, they came with deluges of rain, leaving the courtyard a muddy, slick mess.

On a subsequent occasion at the fence and in similar fashion, Theodor dropped a small bottle of fine perfume in the same pocket. She had mentioned to him in passing that she missed the finer things of womanhood, like makeup, soap and perfume. The simple gesture meant the world to her and she wondered if he sensed the value of the gift.

The distance from the soldiers and prisoners made her plan to be noticed more difficult. How could she stand out if those around her were oblivious to the world around them? She received more acknowledgment from the crow, which she saw daily, usually perched on the same branch. Sometimes when she arrived at the fence the crow was there. If not, it flew in soon after as though it had waited from a distance for her arrival. The crow was definitely aware of her visits, just as was the man in the tower. The crow looked to her often during her stay and rarely left its perch until after she had wandered off to the mess or her sleeping quarters.

The tower soldier hadn't taken long to notice her rapport with the bird. Once, she had imagined his slight smile when the bird flew in to perch while she waited.

A voice from behind her spoke, "He likes you."

Marianne turned abruptly to see Theodor. His uniform was crisp and the rifle hanging from his shoulder glinted in the morning sunlight.

"He's a friendly little fellow," she agreed.

Theodor stood beside her and looked through the fence, then asked, "What do you see when you look into the forest, Marianne?"

Hearing her name spoken brought a breath of freshness. Losing one's identity here is easy, she had learned. "I see the outside."

"And what's outside, your husband?"

His question made her laugh. "Oh gosh, no. I'm not married though I do have a daughter."

"And where is she?"

"Down south," Marianne answered. "Living safely."

"Then you don't belong here. You should be south, raising your daughter."

Marianne stared toward the trees, nodding slowly. "I made a stupid mistake. It won't happen again."

"Are you packed?" he asked.

"Packed for what?"

Theodor pointed toward the tree line and a rummaging squirrel; a gesture apparently meant more for the watching guard than for her. Then he looked to the sky for a long moment. "Pack your things; be ready to go at a moment's notice. I'll let you know when things are in order."

She looked to the sky with him, and asked, "You're talking about escape?"

He ignored the question and said, "I understand that meat is on the menu tonight; beef. It should be good."

Theodor slowly wandered off and under the guard tower then crossed the yard toward the command post office. The crow lifted from the branch, soared directly overhead and crossed the compound, eventually vanishing over the distant treetops.

Marianne turned to glance up to the tower guard. She nodded her goodbye and, as usual, the guard stood motionless while watching her leave.

While she made her way to the mess hall, she sensed the guard's steely eyes watching her. *Does he suspect anything in their conversation?* She wondered. *Be ready to leave at a moment's notice. What in the world does that mean?*

She replayed the conversation in her head while eating her lunch of slop and a crust of bread. The mess hall remained quiet as usual, broken only with haughty conversation among the soldiers. Theodor appeared in the doorway along with two other soldiers before she finished. She watched for him to look her way but he didn't. Instead, he moved slowly through the chow line, engaged in conversation with his companions. They sat at a table that couldn't be farther from hers in the small room.

When finished, Marianne stood from the table, deposited the metal tray, dishes and eating utensils on a table at the front, along with other soiled remnants left by prisoners. She left the hall and moved purposely to her sleeping quarters.

To avoid suspicion from the few prisoners lying in their bunks, while packing the suitcase she tidied up her area, appearing to do little more than light housekeeping. She packed her clothes haphazardly, along with the wash cloth remnants from under her blanket. She set one wash cloth out until she finished cleaning and stowed the suitcase under the bed.

Outside, she tucked the cloth in her pocket and made her way to the water pump. There, she knelt, pumped the handle and trickled water over the cloth to dampen it. While washing, she looked around the compound unsuccessfully for Theodor.

It wasn't until she waited in the chow line that evening that she saw him again. Theodor held his rifle without emotion while overseeing the prisoners entering the mess.

Theodor had been right about the beef on the dinner menu, though it wasn't in the form of steak, or even hamburger. Rather the meat was shredded in a pile and plopped onto her plate just as the servers did with the slop. The server added a ladle of dark green slop though, which resembled mashed peas. She wondered if they knew how to serve any other way. Still, the meat's firm texture and flavor were a welcome departure from the usual gruel. The bread this time came in the form of a hard biscuit. Since the meat and mashed peas had filled the void in her stomach, she dropped the biscuit into her pocket for later.

After eating, Marianne left the mess hall and walked directly to her place along the fence. She waited only moments before the crow flew in to land on the tree branch. He ruffled his feathers and loudly cawed twice, as though calling to her.

The guard stepped from the tower, this time without his rifle. Unusually, he leaned over the rail looking out toward the bird. Standing in such a manner she thought that he looked nearly normal, like a man standing on his front porch to watch the evening sunset.

The crow stood vigil, watching her until she left. Marianne returned to the pump to wash and then ventured to bed.

Over the following three days she saw Theodor only in passing. He made no attempt to acknowledge her, nor did he visit her at the fence where she spent more time in hopes that he would come. *Had he forgotten whatever plan he'd had in mind?* She wondered. Maybe it had only been one of those silly things men say when they find a woman attractive. Life would go on, this mundane life that consisted of steady routine that had kept her somewhat sane.

Then, one evening at dinner time, he approached. His firm gaze seemed to have lost the sparkle that she had so often noticed. His eyes were hard and focused as he stepped close with his rifle in hand and slipped something into her coat pocket. Without a word, he moved past her to inspect the prisoners in line.

Marianne looked to those around her to see if anyone has noticed before slipping her hand into her pocket and feeling a piece of paper.

The line moved forward and she advanced with it.

To avoid suspicion after dinner she ventured to the fence to find the waiting crow. Again, the tower guard leaned over the railing, watching the tree-line.

She lingered only as long as it seemed appropriate before returning to her quarters. The paper in her pocket had piqued her curiosity. When she lay on her bunk, she pulled out the folded paper, opened it and read the scrawled handwriting:

> *Tonight I'll drive a late supply truck into town. Before going to bed set your suitcase at the end of your bunk. I will bed-check the prisoners after dark. When I lift the suitcase, leave the building in front of me and walk directly toward the front gate. Do not speak.*
>
> *At the gate you'll find the truck. Climb into the back and sit quietly. Tell no one of this.*

Her heart raced at the thought of escape. What if they were caught? Escaping prisoners would undoubtedly be shot. And if she did succeed, where would she go? Wherever it was, she would need to get far enough away that searching soldiers wouldn't find her. She was certain that she had had enough of smuggling. The money had been good and oddly, the camp commander had left it in the suitcase. The trains wouldn't be safe after her escape; no form of public transportation would protect her from capture. Aside from being held captive, she hadn't been mistreated beyond the paltry meals and substandard living conditions. At the same time, she held no illusion that she could remain here. She had seen other prisoners trucked from the compound, undoubtedly destined for the massive prisoner of war camps where life was much worse. Remaining here wouldn't do, it must be now or never, she decided.

Now she was restless. Muted evening light shone in through dusty windows. After pulling on her coat, which she rarely wore until daytime temperatures cooled, she hurriedly left the small building and crossed the courtyard, all the while keeping a watchful eye out for Theodor.

Ominous clouds approached over the treetops. The tower guard noticed the threatening storm as she saw him look to the sky. By morning, she suspected, the grounds would become mud soup, unpleasant for spending a day outdoors.

She thrust her hands in her pockets to ward off the evening chill. Until now she had forgotten the three-day-old biscuit she had saved from the beef dinner. She drew the biscuit from her pocket and looked to the guard looking down on her. The crow fidgeted in the branch, a sign she recognized that he was about to lift off. Then, she called out, "Hey, crow!"

The bird fixed its gaze on her. She looked once more to the guard and then stepped several yards back from the fence. She drew back her fist and launched the biscuit over the fence as far as she could throw toward the bird. The bread arced high before descending and plopped into the open field. In one smooth motion, the crow spread its wings and dropped from the tree branch. The bird soared quietly over the field, and then plummeted to snatch up the offering. Marianne heard the wing-beats as it rose higher. The bird cleared the compound fence holding the unbroken bread in its beak and leveled off, soaring until it vanished from her view.

When she looked up to the tower guard she realized that she was smiling as she hadn't smiled in months. For an instant, she caught a gleam in the guard's eye as though he had witnessed something spectacular. Then, he turned and stepped inside the guard tower.

A drop of rain splatted against her face, and then another. She turned and trudged toward the sleeping quarters. Before she reached the door a torrent unleashed on the compound. Inside, she shook off her coat, careful not to wake the sleeping prisoners. Others were there too, those who rarely slept but sat in their bunks staring into a distance where there was no distance. Like her, she knew, they remembered lost freedom and loved ones. Replaying memories of children perhaps like her daughter, Christel, who seemed a world away now.

After shedding her coat and shoes, she slipped the suitcase from underneath the bed and set it at the foot of the narrow bunk. She laid down and propped her hands behind her head thinking of Theodor who, God willing, would arrive in a few hours.

The windows brightened with a lightning flash, and then seconds later a thunder clap shook the small building. This wasn't a night to be outside and she trusted that Theodor wouldn't leave her in the forest.

Marianne startled awake and sat up suddenly when something nudged her foot. Theodor stood over the bed. Even in the dim light she saw his firm gaze, the look of a prison guard not the gentle man she had come to know. He simply nodded and she stood when he lifted the suitcase.

Theodor led her to the door and opened it, then hesitated until she stepped in front of him and outside into the blinding rain. Rain fell in sheets so thick that she was unable to see across the yard.

He followed while she slogged wordlessly through the muck toward the gate entrance. Her eyes searched from side-to-side for anyone that might stop them. They moved close to a guard tower cast in darkness. A shadow moved inside the opening that served as a window without glass. She anticipated a shot which didn't come. After all, her movement across the courtyard wouldn't appear unusual with an armed soldier following her.

The waiting truck materialized suddenly through the rain; a tall, boxed truck similar to the transport that had brought her here. Theodor pulled back the canvas cover over the back and heaved her suitcase onto the bed. Without a word Marianne climbed up inside, moved to the front near the cab and sat on the side bench.

The rain had drenched her. Her hair ran with shedding water and her clothing was saturated clear to her skin. The shoddy boots were mud-covered and soaked.

The truck vibrated when the engine started. In seconds it jolted forward and soon stopped before Theodor had shifted to second gear. Over the rumbling engine she heard him speak with another soldier in Russian. Though she didn't understand the Russian language, the conversation began in normal volume voices, advising the gate guard of his supply run, no doubt. Then, the words became heated and loud.

The one word she did recognize was "Kommandant" which has an identical pronunciation in her native German. Theodor fervently repeated "Kommandant!" Then, the conversation ended abruptly. The engine roared and the truck lurched forward. Each shifting gear caused another jolt as the transport gained speed.

The canvas tarp flapped in the wind. Outside and through the torrent, compound lights grew dim in the distance.

Marianne's internment camp was a little distance outside of Berlin in an area controlled by the Russians. After her arrest in November of 1944, she spent the next few months in the camp. Fortunately for her, the battle for Berlin and Germany raged on away from where she was while Berlin was being ravaged by Soviet troops.

In April 1945, after Marianne had escaped from the prison camp, Hitler committed suicide in his bunker in Berlin to avoid capture and humiliation. After all, Germany had invaded Russia a few years earlier and had inflicted immense pain and suffering on the Russians before the Russian military was able to fend them off and ultimately defeat them— in Russia at last.

On May 2nd, General Helmuth Weidling surrendered Berlin to the Soviets and on May 7, 1945 Germany signed an unconditional surrender and the end of the Third Reich. Marianne was now a free woman and made her way south to seek out her daughter.

## Chapter 9

When I'm outside walking with Romy to feed grain to the pigs, a car drives up the farm driveway. Since it rattles a lot, I hear the car before I see it. People don't often visit us on the farm. When they do, they don't stay long and I usually don't know them. Sometimes other farmers bring work for Herr Ackermann before they leave. He has a machine he calls a welder, and other farmers don't have them, so Herr Ackermann welds steel for them.

I stop in the driveway on my way to the Scheune to see who is coming to visit. The sun is bright making it hard to see who is driving. When the car turns a little bit to park by the house, I see my mama!

"Mama! Mama!" I call out and run toward her.

As soon as Mama steps from the car I run into her legs and wrap my arms around her stomach to hug her.

Mama kneels down and gives me a big hug. Then, she holds me out and looks at my face. It feels so good when she strokes my face and long, brown hair.

Mama says, "Oh, Liebchen, you've grown so! How I have missed you!"

I step in close because I want to hug her all day.

She says, "Your hair has grown so long and beautiful, it feels like silk."

I nod against her shoulder. "Romy says it's from the milk and fresh eggs," I tell her.

I didn't notice the children gathering around until now. Mama stands up and hugs Frau Ackermann and then Romy. She waves to Herr Ackermann who appears briefly in the Scheune doorway before stepping back into the shadows. Herr Ackermann always has lots of work to do in the barn and in the fields.

When the children go back to playing, Mama and I go inside the house with Romy and her mama. Romy pours glasses of milk and slices some cheese to set on the table for my mama and hers. I don't go outside to play with the other children because I want to stay with Mama for as long as she is here.

Romy sets the cheese slices on the table and then sits to listen as Mama tells us stories about where she has been since her last time here. She says she had found some work for the German army but had to quit when she went to something called a prison camp. I've heard of camps for kids, but never one for adult people.

In March of 1946, in the few months since she had escaped from the Russian camp, Mama had lived with a man and his wife in a town outside of the camp. A man named Theodor had helped her escape and helped her to stay with the couple for as long as would be safe. She tells us about her ride across the warfront and back to Berlin. In Berlin she had met with a man named Colonel Gerste and told him she didn't want to smuggle stuff anymore. Since she had been in this camp and didn't like it much, the Colonel told her that was okay. The Colonel added that the "material" wouldn't help much at this point as he sensed the war was almost over and that she should do whatever she could to protect herself from the Russians. He himself had made similar plans. Mama stayed in Berlin until March 1946, doing exactly what, she didn't say other than she had lived in the "American section." After Germany's surrender Berlin had been divided into sections, one each for the United Kingdom, France, United States and Russia.

She later rode the train to Landshut, Germany. She said that Landshut, the capital of the Bavarian district, is nestled in the Alpine foothills on the River Isar. The town is beautiful and peaceful and gave her just the rest she had needed to recover from the imprisonment. Mama liked the city's beautiful Gothic architecture and often walked after work just to look at all the buildings.

Mama got something called a menial job when she got there, and then another job after that. Sadly the first company she worked for had had to close down and the second job wouldn't give her enough money to pay her rent. Mama had been a good secretary before in Berlin, but she couldn't find any more secretary jobs. She started learning English and learned very fast but still spoke with a heavy German accent when she talked to the soldiers. Since she couldn't be a secretary, she moved from her little one bedroom apartment to Fuessen, Germany in 1946, which is in the far south of Germany, just north of a country called Austria. The town borders a mountain range where the people live simple and peaceful. Renting an apartment and furnishings had used up all of her money even though she had been working and would barely allow her to pay for rent and food. She didn't have the money to pay the Ackermann's to keep me on the farm.

Mama asks me, "Are you ready to leave? Will you come with me to Fuessen to live in our new apartment?"

I tell her yes, but I don't really want to go very much. I'm sad because I know I will have to leave Romy. Romy needs me to listen to her talk sometimes. I have lots of friends here from kids my own age up to teenagers. I have never lived anywhere with so many friends before.

She smiles and says that we will find new friends in Fuessen, and that maybe we can come back and visit Romy someday.

Romy stands up, takes my hand and offers to help me pack up my things. She brings two burlap potato sacks to the bedroom. We pull out all of my clothes from the closet and the two dresser drawers that I share with Sabine.

Romy's eyes start to get water in them, and then she sits and pats the bed for me to sit next to her.

She hugs me, "I will miss you so much, Sprite."

Romy hasn't called me Sprite much since Viktor died and it sounds strange to me to hear it again, but I like it.

Romy has been better the last few weeks after she was sad for so long. Sometimes her eyes sparkle again like they used to before Viktor went away. I guess I might not see Romy again for a very long time, but I will never, ever forget her pretty smile.

"Now," Romy says to me, "even though you are leaving, I will think of you every single day."

"I will think of you too," I tell her but it comes out like a whisper. My stomach hurts and something is stuck in my throat.

A tear leaks out of Romy's eye and trickles down her cheek. Her soft hair tickles my face when she hugs me close. She wipes away the tear and says, "Someday we'll see each other again. I hope it won't be too long. You behave for your mama, okay?"

I find it hard to talk so I just nod. Her perfume smells wonderful. This is a smell that I want to remember.

When we finish packing my few clothes and things into the burlap sacks, I carry Baby Anna and Teddy back out to the kitchen. When Mama sees us come in, she stands up from the table.

"All set?" she asks.

Again, I just nod. Romy carries my things outside and we follow her. All of the kids gather around the car. Mama hugs Frau Ackermann and tells her thanks for taking such good care of me. Even Herr Ackermann comes out from the barn and waits to see us go.

After I hug all of the children, Romy kneels and gives me a big hug. Frau Ackermann does the same and says that she'll miss seeing my bright face every day. Sabine stands right next to me the whole time.

Then, I'm surprised when Herr Ackermann lifts me off the ground. He's so strong he lifts me up, and Baby Anna and Teddy all at the same time. His whiskers tickle my cheek like soft sandpaper. He doesn't talk though; he just hugs me and sets me back down.

I can see a bit of Viktor in him, not only in how strong he is but in his blue eyes that look more tired than Viktor's eyes looked. Sabine is the last one to hug me and I will miss her very much. Since she is littler than me, I always tried to take care of her like Romy took care of me. I know that Romy will watch out for her now though and I tell her that.

I kneel and scratch Patch behind his ears. He whines a little and licks all over my face. I think he knows that I'm leaving.

"You're a good friend, Patch." I tell him. "I will miss you very much." Something is stuck in my throat and I hug him around the neck. He smells like a dog, but I want to remember the faint smells of the hay, the cows and the wildflowers in the pasture for as long as I can.

I hold his cheeks in my hands and he looks me right in my eyes. "You take care of the farm, and Romy, okay?"

He whines again, and I think he's trying to say, "okay, I will."

Finally Mama tells me to get into the car. She opens the back door and Patch tries to jump in. I tell him, "No, you can't go." I tug on his collar to get him back out. Then, I get into the car.

I turn around in the seat when the driver turns the car around so I can see all of the kids waving. Romy's eyes are wet and she keeps brushing her cheeks. Herr Ackermann stands next to her, puts his arm around her shoulder and gives her a hug. I've never seen Herr Ackermann hug anybody until today.

The car ride is bumpy even before we get far enough away from the house that I can't see the kids anymore. When we turn the corner onto the road, the kids all start heading back into the barn or the house. I turn around in the seat and try to see over the dashboard but it's easier to look out the side window since the front of the car is so tall.

Mama asks me lots of questions about all the things we did at the farm. I know she does this so I won't be sad, but it doesn't work. I tell her all about Romy and Sabine, and walking to school, and my teacher and some of the things we learned in school. Mama looks proud and listens to everything that I say. Soon we arrive at the train station.

The train ride is very long and even before we come to the first town, I fall asleep. Mama wakes me up when the sun is going down. We stop at a little grocery store and buy sandwiches and a soda that we split between the two of us. Grape soda is one of my favorite things to drink and I try to think back to when I last drank grape soda. It had been in Berlin in our old apartment when Mama had made more money on her paycheck than she thought she would. This grape soda tasted even better than that one though.

When the train starts again, I fall asleep and Mama stays awake almost all the way through the night before we finally get to Fuessen. The apartment is only a short walk from the station and Mama is excited to show me our new home. When she takes me to my bedroom, which has a small bed and a blanket, I lay down with Teddy and my baby and fall asleep.

At this time, in the middle of 1946, Fuessen was occupied by the American Armed Forces. Fuessen had and remains to have, a Panzer (tank) base on the town outskirts which never created a threat to the Allies. Fuessen had been spared the destruction that had befallen other such small, historic, and peaceful towns like Rothenberg. Rothenberg had been destroyed by the U.S. bombers in the last week of the war for no good reason.

Mama and I lived in that apartment until almost Christmas time. Mama couldn't find enough work to pay the rent and I was so mad when the owners of the apartment came one day when we were gone and put all of our stuff outside. They didn't just put our stuff next to the street; they took it all the way to almost out of town and put it by the city cemetery. I don't think they liked Mama very much and I didn't know why.

Christmas comes and we don't get any presents because Santa Claus doesn't deliver presents to people who don't live in houses. My mother had told an American officer that she had no place to stay and they had removed everything. Then, the day after Christmas, four soldiers came to see us in a big truck. They were very mad at the apartment owner for throwing us out. They loaded our stuff into a truck and Mama was so happy that she cried. They took us to an apartment, a really nice apartment that was on the third floor. The apartment had a balcony and we could look out from the balcony and see a beautiful castle.

Mama didn't understand it all, and she told the soldiers she couldn't afford to live anywhere, much less such a nice apartment. After the men moved all of our furniture inside, they told Mama not to worry and gave her a piece of paper and told her to come to that address on Monday morning and to be ready to work.

Mama went to that place on Monday and did secretary work for two American officers. She worked very hard all through the winter and spring, and on July 19, 1946 she took another job at a restaurant called *Baumgarten* in Fuessen/Allgau. Mama still worked for the American officers and worked in the restaurant after she finished that job.

I'm not sure how she did it all, but according to police records from the time, Marianne also worked in Landshut from 5 March, 1946 until 5 May, 1947. During this time she formally divorced my father although this meant nothing to me. I never had a father or a grandfather, uncles, aunts, cousins or any relations that I knew of who survived the war.

I missed my friends at the farm very much, especially Romy and Sabine. I had asked Mama if we could go visit them soon but she said we never had enough money or time, since she worked somewhere every day.

I went back to school of course and it was very hard. The kids there already knew the things I'd learned, and the school was more advanced than the farm school. The teachers taught me every day after school and they worked very hard to teach me all the things I needed to know to keep up with the other kids.

While I mostly liked all of the teachers, one teacher, Frau Koenig became very special to me. I was lucky to have Frau Koenig. She was kind and patient, and took lots of extra time to make sure I understood everything that she taught me. One day she even introduced me to Marga Loeckher, a girl who was my age. Marga and I soon became best friends. She had brown hair and dark eyes and was very pretty. It was good for me to have a friend again who I could talk to. I talk to the teachers and to Mama of course, but no one else understands like another kid.

Marga's house was just a few doors down from our apartment and our apartment was across the street from the *Baumgarten* restaurant where Mama worked. Sometimes I went to Marga's house after school and I stayed there until Mama picked me up after she finished at the restaurant. Marga's mother's name is Maria Loeckher and she and Mama get to be good friends just because Mama got to know Maria when she'd pick me up. I like that Mama and Marga's mama are friends. I don't remember Mama having many women friends before and she seems very happy to have Maria to talk to.

I spend a lot of time with Marga when we walk to school, and go sledding in the winter. I often have dinner there after school and sometimes stay until very late, even on nights when Mama doesn't work at the restaurant. Maria is a good cook since she had to cook in their large fireplace. She used a large pot that swings in and out of the fireplace and her meals are always very good and different. Cooking in the fireplace is cheaper to use than cooking in her small stove that she uses for baking.

Over the months I learn that Marga's family owns a dye business which is also a laundry where people bring their dirty clothes to be washed. When the clothes are ready for pick up the people come back to get their clothes. Marga's father had passed away when Marga was little. Her father used to climb all the mountains in the Alps and died from a heart attack. This made things harder on Maria's family. The oldest boy, Paul, was sixteen-years old. Right now the law says that the oldest boy will inherit all of the businesses and the house that they live and work in. This meant a lot of work for Maria and her five children; Paul, Christoph (nicknamed Bimbi), Jakob (Jacky), Margarete (Marga), and Elizabeth (Lilly).

Christel and Friend in Fuessen, ca. 1947

Once, Marga told me that one of her relatives was taking the family to court to try and take their business and even their house. He didn't think they could do all that work and couldn't keep up with everything. I think she said he was a priest which seemed kind of funny to me. Most priests I ever talked to are nice, this man isn't very nice.

The judge said that Maria and her family could keep the businesses and the house. Mama had tried very hard to help Maria in her court case, and later on Marga told me that actually it didn't help, because my mother went out with a lot of soldiers and worked late nights. She was young and wanted to have good times. This did not look good and people would start gossiping. I don't know why but this made me feel funny and I remembered her words.

The laundry business and dye business was on the ground floor. Maria and Marga's grandmother lived in the first floor apartment and Paul's family, after a few years, lived on the second floor. Jacky lived in another small apartment on third floor. The laundry business was on the right side of the building and above it was still unfinished. A long time ago that area was a barn where the cows would come in from the path that went up to the castle. Marga's family owned all of this and the family worked very hard to keep up with it. The Loeckher family business had existed for a long time and was the only laundry business in Fuessen. The building where Paul and Marga lived had been in continuous use since 1557. The Loeckher family has lived there constantly since 1767.

As the money came in they would fix up the inside of the house for the better. But the law says that they can't change the street side of the houses. The houses have to stay the same. They can only change the facade, but not the structure of the house.

Many times I had dinner over at Marga's house and stayed there. We had a lot of fun. We did homework together, walked together, went sledding, all the good things that friends do.

Not long after my eighth birthday, my mother became good friends with an American soldier. I think she loved him. He brought me chocolates and he brought extra food and he ate dinner with us a lot. Sometimes he took care of me while Mama worked at the restaurant. He always liked to be close to me, especially when Mama was gone. One night Mama came home and she was so very mad at him. As soon as she came in the door she started to yell and pulled me away into the other room. She left the door open though and they both started yelling at each other. Mama picked up a gun and pointed it at him and told him to get out. I hid under the table and had no idea what was happening. I was very scared.

Before the man left, two American soldiers with the letters MP on their arms came and pulled him out of the apartment. When they took him outside, the two American soldiers came back in and talked to Mama. She told them the man was playing games with me that he wasn't supposed to. The next day I heard Mama tell Maria that the MP men took the man to the Army barracks.

## Chapter 10

Over the months and with lots of hard work from myself and the teachers, my schoolwork improved. I made more friends from school but Marga was still my best friend.

As we grew older, our mothers allowed us more freedom from home. First, Marga and I were given permission to walk up and down the street but never cross the streets. Eventually our mothers allowed us to go all the way uptown, which wasn't very far from our apartment. In town we often pretended we were shopping. We had no money but we went inside the shops and looked at all of the pretty things anyway.

One day, after watching a couple of soldiers ask passersby for cigarettes, Marga and I came up with a plan to make some money. We went around the street and picked up all of the cigarette butts that we could find, at least the ones that hadn't been smoked all the way through. We sold the butts to the soldiers on the street for pennies. We thought it was a brilliant plan to make a little money until Marga's mother saw us one day and figured out what we were doing. Of course she told my mother and Mother was very angry.

I was eight-years old and had lived with mother in Fuessen for twenty-four months. Mother worked all the time and couldn't rely on Marga's mother to take care of me so much since she worked all the time too. To avoid future problems created by her working for the Military Occupation Forces and dating American soldiers she decided to enroll me in a convent school in Geimersheim near Ingolstadt. Geimersheim is north of Munich and Munich lies halfway between Ingolstadt and Fuessen. I suppose due to its location, I wouldn't be inclined to run away and return to Fuessen on my own.

I was devastated and Marga cried when they told us. I begged Mother to let me stay with her. I promised I'd behave and not go out anywhere. I would have told her anything to keep from going to a convent, which I really didn't understand much about convents. Mother didn't buy what I was selling. She assured me that I could visit my friends in the summertime but had no intention of letting me stay. I packed my things and left my friends behind again.

Life in the convent was harder than I could have imagined. The only activities available were school and church. We rose each morning at 5 A.M, ate breakfast at 6 A.M., attended church at 7 A.M. School began at 8 A.M. and you never wanted to be late, even if you could find a way. From noon till 2 P.M. we were allowed playtime out in the churchyard and then we had to return and do our homework. Dinner was served promptly at 5 P.M. and the rest of the time we cleaned our rooms, or made something to wear like our stockings or something fit for the church.

We often made fine laces and worked with beads. Attending students consisted of local children as well as the rest of us who lived there. Our main difference was that the local children went home each night and weekend and we stayed. All of the forty-five students, all girls, made beautiful things. In addition, we made all the cloths for the church and even the gowns for the priests.

Our bedrooms were long with at least fifteen beds with two nuns in between us. The nuns' beds were enclosed with curtains to give them privacy while they kept an eye on us. We'd often giggle quietly whenever we heard a nun snore.

On one or two occasions we tried to play hide and seek quietly in the dark. During one such game, I crawled along the floor under the beds and I was hit on the nose with someone's foot. My nose bled freely. I wiped my nose with the drapes and naturally I got into trouble for that.

Soon after, I'd forgotten that punishment. Early one Saturday morning, I became bored and an idea struck me to trick one of the nuns. I attached a very fine and long thread to a small purse. I set the purse on a slippery staircase, watching. When a particular nun descended the stairs and tried to pick it up, I pulled it away. I didn't care much for this nun, Sister Ingona. On her second try when I pulled the purse away, she fell down the stairs. I laughed and gave away my hiding place, but she'd have found me anyway, I suspect. I didn't laugh long because she snatched me up by my ears, dragged me into a

Convent school in Graimersheim near Inglestadt in late 1940's.

classroom and bent me over a desk. She took up a paddle from the side of the room and blistered my behind. This was my first taste of a good paddle spanking for punishment and I hated it. I hated her and swore to never forgive her. The nuns were not gentle. If a student crossed them they often struck the student. Some nuns of course were nice. Sister Marianne was the nicest of all. Short and sweet, she always tried to help me and talk to me. I suspect that she was just as lonely as I was.

The cloister grew most of their own food. They grew all the vegetables and fruit trees bore abundant fruit. The property grew chestnut and hazelnut trees. We gathered honey from beehives, picked pears and apples. Farmers regularly delivered slaughtered animals. All the nuns and girls lifted the

Christel (dark shirt with leg extended) at convent school in Gaimersheim ca. 1948-1949.

pigs with chains into big vats with boiling water to singe off the hairs. Then we scraped with wooden scrapers until the hides were clean. We used almost every part of the body including the intestines to make lamps and even balloons; toys for us to play with. We cooked the chickens, including the bones, into great soups and stews.

We packed good sausages with the leftover meat after the finer cuts were removed. The cloister stored dried milk and an entire cellar full of potatoes.

Some of the lamps we made were really beautiful. During hard times residents from miles around visited the convent to pick up food to hold them over for the winter, or just simply meager times. During the war, we helped people that had been hurt and some who had lost their arms or legs. We all knew that someone had to help them. The visits increased immediately after the war ended.

Our bedrooms had large windows which remained open at night to allow the cool night air inside. Occasionally bats flew in and us girls screamed and covered our heads. The bats would panic and fly willy-nilly to find a way out. One bat tangled itself in a girl's hair. A traumatic ordeal, I thought!

A nun covered the girl's head with a large cloth and two other nuns cut the bat out of her hair. Unfortunately the sisters had to cut away a lot of her hair and she had to attend school that way until it grew back decently. While I don't remember her ever recovering from the bat, attending school with her hair cut away in chunks must have been equally devastating.

To keep us healthy, the nuns also gave us regular doses of cod liver oil. Despite the oil, I stayed healthier than the other girls because I ate everyone's left overs; especially the vegetables that no one liked. I had learned to like vegetables on the farm and have always enjoyed them since.

True to my adventurous and curious nature, I once discovered a pathway that led from the cloister across the yard into the garden. On more than one occasion I took a couple of the girls with me as we snuck out and ate vegetables and berries. And of course we were discovered and I was punished again.

We occasionally helped neighboring farmers when they had trouble with bugs infesting the potatoes and vegetables. At times the fields were overrun by potato beetles. Often the entire school traveled out to pick those beetles off the plants. We each were given a glass jar with a top. The jars contained a bit of gasoline to kill the bugs.

Sometimes on the weekends we rode a bus to the forest to pick wild mushrooms. Picking mushrooms was my favorite pastime. Just the opportunity to be away from the school and enjoy the fresh mountain air made the work worth it; and picking wild mushrooms was relatively easy work.

For discipline purposes, the nuns had devised an archaic system. If someone took anything that didn't belong to them, and the nuns couldn't figure out who did it, they passed a slip of paper to each student.

A sister had drawn a cross on only one paper and, of course, the one who received the cross was guilty. I suppose their faith in God delivered the thief in such a manner. I received that cross numerous times, even on the occasions when I was innocent.

During my time at the convent, Mother became friends with a WAC, (Women's Army Corps.) a female Army officer named Captain Helen Magoon. She'd met Captain Magoon in the restaurant since many American soldiers ate at the *Baumgarten* and I suppose it was just a matter of time until these two met.

Soon after their friendship formed, Helen became quite sick in the hotel where she stayed. Since no one seemed interested in helping her get medicine, Mother brought her medicine and food from the *Baumgarten* restaurant.

Helen was so grateful for mother's help that she began to send me suitcases full of food when she felt well enough. When her first suitcase arrived, I was baffled of course, until I read her letter of explanation. I opened a subsequent suitcase that followed a few weeks later and it scared me half to death! When I opened the lid, an animal face looked out at me!

This ball shaped animal head consisting of hair with two eyes set the nuns to laughing. They explained that it was a coconut, which I'd never seen in my young life.

I regularly shared my bounty of spam, chocolate and gum with the other girls. I began to call her "Aunt Helen" since, as far as I knew, she had no other family.

All of us girls learned a lot of patience and perseverance which certainly helped me throughout life. Even though school was difficult,

I am grateful for the experience because it must have been a chore for Mother to pay for schooling in the cloister.

I always enjoyed coming home and of course, I missed my mother and my best friend, Marga. I tried to escape the convent three times. Each time though I was caught and each time I was punished. On my last escape attempt I rode a bus all the way home to Fuessen. Mother was unhappy when I arrived and immediately arranged to have me returned to the convent.

The following summer I returned home to visit and Marga and I made up for lost time. We visited castles called *Neuschwanstein* and *Hohenschwangau*. Parades and shows were held often in Fuessen and of course we spent time in the beautiful mountains where we rode the gondolas. We bicycled and got together with a lot of different friends. Much of Marga's time was required at the laundry though, ironing laundry and sometimes her mother allowed me to help her.

The business and the house had become stressful for Maria. Aside from the laundry duties, Paul also had to learn the accounting books and keep all the machines running. Much of the laundry had to be delivered to various restaurants and to the regular customers. Many sports clubs also brought in a lot of the business. The most business for the laundry in the past had come from the German Army and now they received a lot of business from the Occupation army. Paul picked up uniforms, linens and other items daily, brought them to the laundry business and then returned them, fresh and clean.

Soon, I returned to the convent to begin another school year.

A year later in 1950, when I had been in the convent for two years, unbeknownst to me, Mother and Captain Helen began to make other plans. Aunt Helen had received a transfer to Nürnberg, (Nuremberg), Germany. She had also arranged for my mother to work in a General's offices in Furth, outside of Nürnberg. This job would pay so well that one job would provide the income she needed. When they informed me of the move, I was excited for Mother to only work one job and as a secretary, which she loved. However, I knew that Nürnberg was a long way from Fuessen and my best friend, Marga.

Christel taking the train to Fuessen, 1949

Mother moved to Nürnberg on 28 September, 1950 and I spent my summer with her. I had always missed Marga while I was in the convent, but the convent kept me so busy it wasn't difficult. Now, with no friends and little to do, I missed her terribly.

I often played in the yard outside at Mother's apartment when I was there. When a man came by to visit my mother one day, I paid little attention to him but before he left, he came to the backyard and watched me play for a few minutes. He stepped down from the porch to approach me, and then he asked, "Do you know me?"

At first I thought this was an odd question. I shook my head and answered, "No, I don't." His presence startled me and I looked around for my mother.

Then, he asked, "Are you happy?"

As soon as I told him that I was very happy, he suddenly turned and left. I ran into the house and asked my mother, "Who was the man who was just here?"

My mother bent over me, took my hands and answered, "That was your father."

I was shocked! When the shock wore off I remembered looking into the man's eyes and had noticed that they were blue, and quite sad. I returned to the backyard to play with little thought about the father I had just met and had never known. That is my only first-hand memory of my father.

When summer ended, I returned to the convent. Since Mother now lived in Nürnberg, she thought it best that I leave the convent and attend a Protestant school that was closer to home, which I did in 1951. This also meant changing my religion from Catholic to Protestant. Since I'd never been given a choice about religion, I suppose it mattered little to me.

The Protestant School was nice and the teachers were much friendlier. They taught no religious classes. Instead, we learned acting, dancing and sports. I enjoyed the environment tremendously. Still, Nürnberg was far from my best friends, Marga and her family.

Captain Helen often came to visit. She and Mother frequently drank coffee in the kitchen after work. I was in the kitchen pouring a glass of milk when I heard them mention traveling to the United States. I knew the United States from school and it sounded like a wonderful place full of hope, where anyone could find a dream. This confused me somewhat as I had written a letter, of which I had written few to my mother, regarding her association with the American soldiers. Were these soldiers our enemies or our friends?

Christel's 1950's school picture before moving to Nürnberg.

Captain Helen and Mama said little more after that though, so I went about my business.

A year later, together they told me one evening that they were planning to move to the United States and that my time at the Protestant school was limited. This sounded like an exciting adventure.

I was now eleven-and-a-half years old and time flew by. I hadn't made any close friends since I knew I would leave school soon.

Aunt Helen made all the arrangements for us to leave for the United States. She booked us on the *S.S. New Amsterdam*. This ship would depart from Rotterdam, Holland. The idea excited me now, it seemed so real, and we had all heard that in America life was easier and better than in Germany. I hoped I would make new friends. We would find a nice house to live in and I'd attend a new school.

The idea seemed so magical that I feared Mother might change her mind.

At times, my mother was an enigma, no one really knew for certain what she would do. Not even Mother, I suspect. I knew that she'd miss her friends at the Stammtisch. When you visit a pub often enough, eventually the proprietor awards you with a Stammtisch, your own table. The regulars all sat nightly at the same table where they talked about who knows what. This alone could be enough for Mother to cancel the whole adventure at any second.

Christel with friends in Nürnberg

Events moved in a whirlwind when I left school. We packed and stored or gave away all of our belongings and left for the shipyard. The day had arrived and Mother hadn't yet changed her mind. Still, I kept a wary eye on her, we hadn't set sail yet.

Mother had been unusually quiet on the drive to the Rotterdam docks where Captain Helen met us. The look in Mother's eye and her lack of excitement did little to convince me that we were actually about to board a ship.

We stepped from the car and hugged Aunt Helen. She, at least, instilled some excitement and confidence in my wary mother. Aunt Helen's transfer would still take a while, and when it arrived she intended to fly on a military transport to the States.

We unloaded our bags and carried them toward the *S.S. New Amsterdam*. Not until we'd come close enough to read the name on the bow would I believe that this massive vessel would carry us across the ocean. The decks stretched so high that I craned my neck to see to the top smokestacks. It would take several minutes or longer, even walking at my fastest pace, to walk the length of the ship. Big! Beautiful! Magnificent! Words couldn't describe this!

We hugged Aunt Helen and left her on the dock before towing the luggage up the gangplank. We, along with other passengers, were dressed in our finest clothes. The women looked elegant wearing fine jewelry and fox furs; the men handsome, some even wore tuxedoes. Of course, some passengers were also servicemen and women, all adorned in their dress blues.

The boarding looked like more of a party than an ocean crossing. Everyone smiled, laughed and talked a mile a minute. Everyone, it seemed was as enamored with this massive vessel as I was; except for Mother.

I watched Mother closely when we made it to the deck and stopped so the crewman could examine her paperwork. She appeared uncertain; this had been be my worst fear. We had come too far to have her snatch it all away now. I imagined the embarrassment if she turned, led me back down to the dock and back to Nürnberg.

When the crewman approved our papers, he welcomed us aboard.

## Chapter 11

Mother and I soon located our cabin. Mother thought certainly there had been some mistake as our large and elegant cabin was a first class cabin. Aunt Helen had secretly asked for a first-class upgrade and the Holland American Line had obliged since they hadn't filled the first class section.

The room was magnificent with two beds, a small dining table and three portholes on the bulkhead for us to look out of. I have never felt so lucky in my life.

When we had unpacked our clothes and stored them in the closet and dressers, we stepped out the cabin door and watched over the railing until the last passenger had boarded. We soon spied Aunt Helen at the front of the gathered crowd, waving frantically. We called to her but I'm not sure that she heard us. She shouted back and we couldn't make out her words.

Every passenger came out on deck to wave and call their goodbyes to family and friends waiting on the dock. This was an event unlike anything I had witnessed or imagined.

The crew lifted off the gangplank and soon after cast off the mooring lines. The ship slowly moved forward and away from the dock. Quietly, I breathed a sigh of relief. We watched the crowd until Aunt Helen seemed to just blend in with all the other faces.

When the noise of the distancing crowd had died down, we returned to our cabin and dressed for dinner. Mother helped me pick out my nicest outfit, which she and Aunt Helen had bought for this occasion. The blue satin dress fit perfectly. Matching shoes and even a handbag, which I'd never owned before, completed the ensemble.

We left the cabin and walked the decks to one of several dining halls. When we stepped inside the room, I was speechless. The walls glistened with fine stained oak. Chandeliers hung high overhead. The dining tables were draped with white linens and cloth napkins, fine china and crystal glasses. We were seated at a table of eight people including the two of us.

Christel, (far left) and Marianne, (second from right) on the New Amsterdam, April 1952

Every woman in the room glittered with jewelry. The men wore tuxedoes. Everyone including Mother and I looked so nice. I knew the ship was underway but I could hardly feel it move. We floated along peacefully. The experience of the ship and the dining room were both exciting and soothing.

Even at my young age I knew that the passengers, though they all looked of equal class, likely came from all walks of life. No one here could know of our tumultuous life, just as we were unaware of their vocation or background. Here everyone, if for just a short week, could appear wealthy and refined. Perhaps this is why the journey seemed such a celebration for each and every passenger that I encountered over the coming days.

After dinner, Mother and I were so tired from packing and the trip to the docks that we went right to bed. After all, the trip would require six days and nights, plenty of time for me to see everything.

Since Mother felt a little seasick the next morning, I spent the day exploring the entire boat. It was definitely a king-sized ship and had been well-built. I toured the galley, the engine room, the movie theater, the swimming pool, several shops, three different spas, and the game rooms; all were unimaginably magnificent.

During the evening, and each subsequent evening the ship produced huge shows. Like the dining room, the showrooms were adorned with fine oak wood and magnificent lamps and chandeliers.

Although my mother's mild seasickness continued I never experienced it. Despite the illness, every evening Mother went dancing and had a lot of fun with some of the people she had met. In between she would get nauseous.

I often played a horseracing game on deck. The game pieces were small numbered statues of horses. Whenever I called out numbers of different horses, the horses advanced. I thought this was a great game as I won often.

In the evening while Mother prepared to dine and dance, I visited the ship's captain in the wheelhouse who was kind enough to teach me about the different instruments and gave me a full tour of the bridge.

I returned frequently to visit the Captain in the wheelhouse. I especially enjoyed the evenings when the sea was quiet and the only lights came from the stars or a rare passing ship in the distance.

On most days the ship glided silently over still water but we also had days when the waves kicked up and rocked the ship to and fro. On those days, Mother's seasickness worsened of course, but her overall health wasn't a concern.

On one particular day when the waves were higher than usual, I swam in the pool and didn't really have to swim. I would stay in one place and the motion from the waves carried me from one end of the pool to the other. That is, until the waves had made swimming unsafe. The crew closed the pool and we had to get out. As an extra precaution they even drained the pool since the pool contained saltwater and would cause a mess if it slopped over the decks.

For six days and nights we sailed seeing nothing but sky and ocean all around us. Then, at approximately 5 A.M. on April 24th, 1952 the Statue of Liberty came into view. Battling a particularly bad bout with the churning sea in her stomach, Mother even ventured from the cabin to see Lady Liberty. I smiled wide and stood next to her, happy to share this moment together.

Since the S.S. New Amsterdam docked in New York Harbor on April 24th, 1952; this made me almost twelve years old. Tomorrow, the 25th would be my twelfth birthday. At twelve-years-old, Aunt

Helen would have had to pay for a full fare, adult ticket. My child fare had been half of the adult cost. To me, this was my lucky day and defined my destiny, to arrive in America for a memorable birthday celebration.

We arrived at the dock in New York. Confusion was everywhere. Suitcases and people were all in the hallways waiting to get off the ship. Finally we lined up and showed our passports and documents to the authorities again. My mother seemed nervous as she anxiously tried to find out where to go and where the taxis were. The ship's porters brought down our suitcases, hailed us a taxi and then even helped the cabbie load them into the taxi. The cab pulled away from the docks and when it turned onto the New York City streets our eyes bulged. Both of us looked up to see the sky between the tallest buildings that I could have ever imagined.

We arrived at the hotel, checked in and settled into our room. As was Mother's way, we set out our clothing for the following morning, because it was my birthday and Aunt Helen had arranged for us to visit Radio City Music Hall and then attend a film titled, *North by Northwest*.

A day after the most wonderful birthday that I'd ever had, we boarded a train to Worcester Massachusetts. Suddenly, on the train my mother began to cry. I suppose all of the changes that came with traveling so far, and the unknown future began to catch up with her. Some years later I brought up the incident and she mentioned that we had passed a train station with the sign *Berlin, Connecticut* and this had been too much for her to take.

Now, in this country I found it interesting that everyone spoke English and only English. I didn't understand a word of it but Mother did her best to continuously translate for me.

When we finally arrived in Worcester, two ladies met us at the station. Aunt Helen, Captain Helen Magoon, had made arrangements for two of her friends to look after us until she transferred back to the States to Fort Devens, Massachusetts which is just outside of Worcester.

The ladies seemed nice and were quite friendly. Dr. Minerva Zehner, was a doctor with a practice in downtown Worcester. The other woman who was much older, I later learned was her mother. Dr. Zehner drove us to their house which was very nice. Her large backyard was laden with rosebushes. Since her mother required assistance just getting around the house, our job was to help her whenever we could. I enjoyed helping her since I needed to learn English quickly, and what she didn't teach me I learned by watching television all day and half the night.

Mother soon enrolled me in school and with my paltry understanding of the language my grades in the beginning were all 'F's. As my study of English improved, so did my grades. Math was my favorite subject because numbers were easy to pick up and mentally translate into my native German.

My mother landed a job at the gun factory and, as was her way, she worked long hours to earn money. Before we knew it, Aunt Helen arrived from overseas and we made arrangements for our own apartment.

We moved into Number 8, Bowdoin Street, Worcester, Massachusetts. No sooner were we moved in than Aunt Helen was required to report for duty at Fort Devens, which is also in Massachusetts. She reported for work and would also live on base.

My mother and I lived alone in the three bedroom apartment. All the rooms were on the ground floor and we had a huge back yard. We did our best to keep the yard nice as this was Mother's escape from her long hours at work.

Ever since Marga's comment about my mother and men, the thought always stuck in my mind. Before Marga had mentioned it long ago, I hadn't noticed that Mother was different from any of my friends' mothers. We attended a local church, which gave me the opportunity to practice English and to make new friends. Mother often had to work on Sunday so she didn't always accompany me on the short walk to the services. On one particular Sunday after the service, a priest stopped me outside and asked how Mother and I were doing.

I told him that we were fine, but then I also confided that Mother had several male friends, who visited often and that I didn't like it. I had become uncomfortable with the idea of the frequent visitors and what my friends or the neighbors might think.

Two days later the Priest came to our house and stood on the porch speaking with my mother through the door. I listened secretly from the hallway. When he questioned her about the men, I became sick to my stomach from nervousness. I truly regretted confiding in him.

Mother grabbed him by the collar, pushed him backward and told him that her visitors were none of his business nor was anyone who came and went from her home. The priest nearly tumbled backward down the steps and nearly ran back to his car. I never saw him again near our house or even at church.

Of course, Mother was angry with me and hit me several times until she was satisfied that I had gotten the message. Six months later I attributed this punishment to her decision to return to New York City, alone. She said she wanted to found her own business to sell imported cloth and patterns. She returned me to live with Dr. Zehner and her mother until summer when Aunt Helen had invited me to Fort Devens to live with her. So it was that after only a few months in Worcester, she took off again without me. Worcester was just too small. Mother was a Berliner and she needed room to operate. She intended to open a textile business, she said. New York City should suit her style just fine and the German community in and around East 86th street would be her command post.

Bicycling around Fort Devens one afternoon I experienced a sharp pain in my side. The pain was so intense that I left the bike and walked into the house. Aunt Helen rushed me to the hospital in Worcester. A doctor examined me and said that I had appendicitis and my appendix had burst.

Mother immediately flew in from New York for my operation. Back in the 1950's of course, medical technology was such that an appendix operation left me with big scars and I never again wore a two-piece bathing suit.

After the operation I returned to live with Dr. Zehner and her mother and the summer passed quickly. The living situation saved my life when I contracted rheumatic fever not long after I returned to school and the doctor diagnosed and treated me with medication early enough that it didn't affect my heart, which is nearly always the case.

It was during this period while living in Worcester and my mother being in New York City that a strange thing happened. At least it seemed strange to me as I had no idea what she was doing regardless of what she had told me given her past activities in Germany.

In December of 1953, about eighteen months after our arrival in the States, a letter arrived at our old address at 8 Bowden Street. The letter was addressed to Mother and had been sent from George E. Meloon, (nearly spelled like Magoon,) Personnel Director, The Central Intelligence Agency in Washington, D.C. inviting my mother to apply for a position, since she was: "a person who may be qualified for a position with the Central Intelligence Agency."

This was an invitation from the Personnel Director himself. Because of the vetting process in Germany to attain her visas to immigrate to the U.S. in a relatively short time, they surely knew more about her than she might have known about herself.

I wondered how she had been able to obtain permission to travel to the U.S. in such a short time, given the events in Germany at the time. Did Major Helen Magoon and the U.S. Army have plans for her that I knew nothing about? Did the episode with the mercury and the Russians have anything to do with this? It's interesting that the C.I.A. was formed from the O.S.S.– the clandestine intelligence agency in the U.S. Army during WWII. (I expect now, many years later, I may never know the answer to these questions since my mother and Major Helen Magoon have now passed.) I never knew what my mother was doing most of the time, however, I knew she was capable of almost anything.

In 1955, and after three years I had done well in school and auditioned for a seat in a better school, the Classical High School in Worcester. I passed their examinations and was accepted, which made me quite proud since I hadn't even spoken English when I had first arrived in America.

I'm not sure what was on my mother's mind at this time when she told me to come 'home' to New York to live with her. Just when I had begun to find my feet again, she decided to pull me out of school. She gave me no choice but to pack up and meet up with her in New York since she already had enrolled me in the *Julia Richman High School* on the Upper East Side. The school is located at East 67th Street and Second Avenue. Everything moved faster there. Hallways and classrooms were much more crowded and the students were frequently rude. I didn't like the school.

Our gym teacher once asked that while she stepped out for a moment, that I have all the girls line up in rows. She said she'd return momentarily. Here I am, the new girl asking the girls to line up. Some ignored me, others laughed, and some even threatened to beat me up after school. I was terrified! After class I went to the school office, called Mother and asked her to pick me up, which she did.

The following day, she enrolled me in *Rhodes High School*, a private school. What a difference a day makes. The students were friendly and the teachers were helpful. I was particularly excited to see a sign in each classroom which read "Every class is an English class". *Rhodes High School*, or sometimes known as *Rhodes Preparatory School* was so much more than a high school. This was the precursor to college for many well-known businessmen, actors and politicians, something I didn't realize at the time.

More importantly to me, the school was located at 11 West 54th Street which is just a short distance from the *St. Patrick's Cathedral*. I enjoyed spending time at the cathedral, often stopping after school to do my homework.

I soon made a number of friends, which included three boys who often accompanied me to do homework. During our free time we walked the Manhattan streets. We walked; we talked, sometimes buying treats or hot dogs when one of us had the funds.

Our friendship grew strong until our high school prom approached and I was forced to choose which of the three boys to go with. Through much distress, I finally chose Albert, a nice and gentle boy who I'd grown very fond of. Albert was smart and did well in school.

The prom was everything I'd dreamed and I owe that memory to my date. In the weeks after prom, Albert and I became an item of sorts. We visited *Central Park* and the zoo. He took me to see a show called *Madam Butterfly*, which was sad but I enjoyed it immensely. The music was especially good. Traditionally the *Rhodes School* graduation was held at the *Waldorf Astoria* where, after graduation, we danced through the night and ate breakfast the following morning with our parents.

Of course, earlier I'd been nervous to have my mother to breakfast in such a fine hotel, given that I never knew what she might say or do. God forbid she would embarrass me in front of Albert and his parents. But, she showed up in fine style and the breakfast went off without a hitch. As I mentioned, I never knew what Mother might say or do.

Albert had once confided that his folks didn't approve of him seeing me. Unfortunately, soon after, Albert decided that medical school, and taking over his father's medical practice was in his future. I never saw him again.

My mother and I currently lived in a New York apartment at 339 E.86th Street. Mother enjoyed the area since it was always quite busy. The apartment was also centrally located, close to *Schultzen Park* and *Doctor's Hospital* where Mother worked. Of course, East 86$^{th}$ Street is the Germantown area boasting several top German Restaurants including *Schaller and Weber*, a German meat shop and *The Bavarian Inn Restaurant*. Mother and I frequented *The Bavarian Inn*, in particular.

One late afternoon after I had finished my studies and college applications I walked to *Schultzen Park*, which I visited as often as I could. I continued on past the Governor's house and then met up with my Mother outside of the Hospital. I had never gone inside of the hospital, she always met me outside. On this particular day, I noticed a flurry of activity. People were rushing in and out more than usual. Newspaper and television photographers anxiously milled about outside the front doors on the concrete sidewalk.

Finally my Mother showed up and we began walking toward The Bavarian Inn, as we had so many times before. I asked her about all the excitement at the hospital.

She said, "Marilyn Monroe was admitted today."

"Really?" I asked. "What happened to her."

She smiled softly and answered, "She had a special miscarriage."

"Oh, that's terrible!" I said and we continued walking. Mother never mentioned the incident again.

During dinner at the inn, Mother introduced me to one of the waiter's and his wife, who had been quietly occupying a corner table during our dinner. The woman was in a wheelchair and she looked very weak. She wore an eye patch and it was apparent that she had taken great pains to look nice that evening.

Her husband and our waiter, Heinz was considerably handsome. His smile turned on at each table that he attended, and he was friendly toward me, and to Mother.

When he had left our table, Mother told me that his wife, the woman in the wheelchair, had been stricken with cancer. The eye patch concealed where one eye had been surgically removed. I admired Heinz' dedication to her as he often stopped at her table to chat, or to bring her whatever she needed. I felt quite sad for the both of them, anticipating that she didn't have long left in this world..

Following dinner we returned to our apartment and I continued my studies. It was quite a stressful time for me because I had to be sharp since I wanted desperately to be accepted into *Notre Dame College* on Staten Island.

Soon after High School graduation in 1959, I was accepted to *Notre Dame* for premed curriculum. In searching for a place to live, and somewhere not far from college, I answered an ad posted at school. After a phone call, Mrs. Vivianne Kuhrt consented to show me the room.

When I boarded the *Staten Island Ferry*, the day had become cloud covered and rain soon began to fall. I hadn't thought to bring an umbrella. By the time I made it from the ferry to the bus, the rain poured and I was drenched to the bone.

When I stepped down from the bus a young man stretched out his hand and smiled wide, then he asked, "Are you Christel?"

I nodded 'yes' as he held the umbrella up to shield me from the downpour.

"My name is Peter," he said. "My aunt, Mrs. Kuhrt, worried about you in the rain, so she asked me to come with the umbrella and take you to see the room."

I smiled, and I'm sure I stammered a few words while thinking, *my, he's a nice young man!*

Peter and I walked the streets beneath the umbrella, chatting to pass the time. We arrived and he introduced me to his aunt, Mrs. Vivianne Kuhrt, who showed me the room. The room was cozy and comfortable, not too extravagant but was just what I needed for privacy to study. We came to an agreement on the rent and when exactly I could move in, which needed to be soon.

When college time arrived a week later, Peter had been on my mind. I moved in and stored all of my clothes in the dresser and closet. Peter often came by the house to wash his car, and even took Mrs. Kuhrt and me to dinner occasionally.

Before I knew it, the semesters had finished and I stayed on the island to attend summer school. Since *Notre Dame College* didn't have summer programs, I enrolled in the *Wagner College* summer program where Peter was attending. Since *Wagner College* was just down the street from *Notre Dame*, I took up residency in the girl's dorm.

Even while at the dorm, Peter and I dated in the evenings, but the girls had to be back at the dorm by 11 P.M. Of course, Peter and I found time to be alone away from the dorm. I think it had become obvious to everyone who knew us that I had fallen hard for Peter. I looked forward to spending time with him. I began to appreciate how handsome he was. His good looks came from deep inside of his kind soul. He displayed gentleness with everyone and I admired and respected him. He certainly showed respect for me and for all that I was trying to accomplish. More than any boy I'd ever dated, Peter had a sense of responsibility.

To be fair he was a little older than I was and had been in the Air Force for four years and had just been discharged in August of 1959, a few weeks before his Aunt Vivienne had asked him to meet me at the bus stop.

After a few months in the dorm, I began feeling poorly every morning and soon realized that I may have become pregnant. My head hung low the night I walked out to the parking lot to meet Peter. My stomach was unusually upset and my legs felt like two logs dragging beneath me.

The night was unusually cool and I drew my coat tight when I approached his car. As was his way, he stepped from the car, beaming a bright smile when he called my name.

I fell into his arms and just held him close. He held me for a moment and then tucked a finger under my chin, urging me to look up to him. "What's happened now?" he asked.

I suspected that he thought something had happened with my mother again, which seemed to occur often. I shook my head slowly, and answered, "I'm afraid I may be pregnant."

Peter's smile only wavered slightly when he pulled me in close. "Don't worry about a thing. If it's true, we'll figure it out."

## Chapter 12

New York City in the fall offers certain magic to those in love. Hot summer days give way to cool breeze and even cooler evenings. Show-house lights glitter like diamonds and music plays endlessly. Steam rises from vendor carts on every street corner; the smells advertise everything from great hot dogs and hot pretzels to Irish sausages and pirogies. New York City is such a melting pot that a person can visit every culture in the world simply by visiting its boroughs.

Despite the magic I felt, Mother never liked Peter from their first meeting. In all fairness, from September of 1959 when I first met Peter, through 1960 and up until the times I told her of my condition she had only met him once or twice and I never told her of my involvement with him. It might have been a shock to her having gone through all that she had in the last twenty-years, only to have her only daughter tell her that life would change in a way that she had never wanted for me.

Now, two months later, her feelings hadn't changed. After visiting the doctor who confirmed my pregnancy, Peter and I knew we must travel to New York to tell my mother about our plan to marry. We agreed to first tell her about the wedding, news of the baby could wait until later.

I'm unclear why Mother never liked Peter. It may have been his carefree, upbeat attitude or his tendency to embrace whatever life delivered. And he always made the best of life. He wasn't one to complain or begrudge his want for anything, he simply played the cards he'd been dealt. Or it may be the attention he directed toward me, which robbed Mother of my time spent with her.

Shortly after our arrival in New York, Mother's reaction to the news had been neither for nor against the marriage. She never voiced her opinion; a most unusual reaction from her. Mother had always had an opinion about everything; I suppose this should have been a red flag to me.

Peter's mother began arranging for the wedding. She booked the church and, after much discussion, reserved *The Meurot Restaurant* for the reception. Her excitement was intoxicating. She single-handedly transformed the impending nuptials from a promise to reality. Mother even caught the fever and soon accompanied me while shopping for flowers, and other necessary arrangements.

Mother and I spent days shopping for just the right dress and soon purchased my dream dress. I couldn't have been happier sharing these moments with Mother as she seemed to have come around quickly.

In reality Mother had other plans, as I should have known. Plans that would take a very dangerous and unpredictable path.

Between wedding plans, Peter and I searched, and finally found a one-bedroom apartment directly across from *Wagner College*, the college where Peter was attending.

Mother currently lived at 339 East 86th Street. One cold and late September day I arrived at Mother's apartment to find her boyfriend, Heinz Hofmann. While with my mother at dinner one previous evening, we had seen Heinz at the *Bavarian Restaurant* between Third and Lexington Streets, just one block from our new apartment. Heinz Hoffman had immigrated to the U.S. in 1956 from Köln (Cologne) Germany with his wife and took up residence in the 86th street area of New York City, aka: Germantown or Steuberville named after the revolutionary war hero from Germany. After living in the States for a year or two, his wife was diagnosed with incurable cancer and she asked Heinz to return with her to her homeland to die, which he did in approximately 1959.

Mother and I had met Heinz a few times at the *Bavarian Inn* where he worked as a waiter, along with his wife who came occasionally to wait for him to finish work. After his wife's death he returned to New York and resumed his work at the inn. By 1960 while I was away at college, Mother and Heinz had become a couple but I had no idea about any of this.

I greeted Heinz and he invited me inside.

*Marianne and Heinz Hoffman at The Bavarian Restaurant*

I removed my coat just as Mother entered from the kitchen. She paused in her step and appeared concerned. She approached and studied me closely. "You look different somehow," she said.

I asked, "Different?"

"Yes, different. Is it your hair?" she shook her head, "No, I think you've gained a bit of weight."

"Have I?" My palms moistened and my heart raced. "It could be. We've been so busy I hadn't noticed."

A mischievous twinkle was in her eye when she nodded, knowingly. "Well, no matter. Sit, have some tea." She motioned toward the kitchen.

Over tea we discussed details for the wedding. Mother seemed distant and not as attentive as she had recently been about the wedding. Then, she said, "I thought it would be splendid to arrange for a coach, drawn by two white horses to drive you and Peter from the church to the reception."

"A coach? No, in Germany maybe but not on Staten Island. What would people think?"

Mother's face flushed. "Well, they'll think it's the grandest thing they'd ever seen!"

"No, Mother," I insisted firmly. "I'd like this to be an American wedding, in America."

"Just because they have coaches in Germany doesn't mean you can't have one in America! This *is* an American wedding; just add a touch of German culture, that's all I ask."

"A coach would overrun what we've planned so far. No coach, no German culture. Let's just go with what we have planned."

Mother unwillingly relented. We finish our tea and I stood from the table telling her that I needed to get home for school tomorrow and I still had so much to do for the wedding.

Mother walked me to the door and helped with my coat.

She kissed my cheek when Heinz opened the door. "Take care of yourself," she said. "You look tired."

"I'm fine," I told her. "I'll see you next weekend."

While walking down the apartment staircase, I knew that she had sensed my pregnancy. She seemed withdrawn and not nearly as excited about the wedding as she had in the previous weeks. Mother had more on her mind than a simple horse drawn carriage and the thought made me uneasy. I vowed to tell her about the baby on my visit next weekend.

The days passed quickly with schoolwork, stolen moments with Peter and finalizing wedding plans, which was now a mere two weeks away. At times it seemed I'd never get everything done, and all the while Peter assured me that the details didn't matter. We would be married and that was the most important part of any wedding.

I returned to Mother's late Friday evening to a quiet apartment. I wore loose fitting clothing as my belly had begun to swell, and if Mother had doubted my pregnancy the week before, she surely wouldn't now.

I supposed that Mother had gone out to dinner, perhaps an evening of drinks with friends. Feeling sleepy after the long week, I went to my small bedroom to nap. It was after dark when I heard Heinz and her come in the front door, and soon, she opened the door to my bedroom and entered.

"Good evening, liebchen," she said when she sat on the bed and stroked my hair.

Mother hadn't called me liebchen for years it seemed, and I liked the sound of it.

"You look tired," she said. "Are you getting enough rest?"

I admitted that I hadn't slept well but don't tell her it's largely due to the baby. I struggled to sit up and told her that I'd get something to drink.

She laid a hand on my chest, gently pressing me back down on the bed. "You rest. I'll get you something to drink." Then she left the bedroom and returned just moments later. She handed me a glass of soda and two small white pills. "Here, take these, they'll help you sleep. I'll draw you a bath."

"What are they?" I asked before she left the bedroom.

She called quietly over her shoulder, "just aspirin. Take them."

I realized that I was more tired than I had imagined. I popped the pills into my mouth and drank half of the soda to wash them down. I laid back on the bed listening to the water run in the tub just across the hallway.

My legs and arms began to feel weak and rubbery. Mother returned and I told her that I didn't feel well.

She helped me from bed and almost had to carry me to the bathroom. "A warm bath will fix you up," she said. "Then you'll sleep well tonight and feel like brand new in the morning."

My legs and arms were numb making it impossible to undress and get into the bath without her assistance.

She said, "relax you will feel better soon." She repeated this over and over.

Her voice seemed to be so very far away, almost as though I was dreaming. My thoughts clouded making the room seem hazy and surreal. I wondered, *What is wrong with me?* I was concerned that something must be wrong with the baby.

Then, she raised her voice almost to a scream. Her words made no sense in my subconscious state but she was clearly angry. Through hazy vision I saw her stand over me with a wire coat hanger.

She knelt next to the tub and bent over me. "Don't you dare tell anyone of this or I will be arrested!"

Burning pain between my legs was unbearable. I screamed, "Someone help me! Mother, what are you doing? MOTHER!"

I heard Heinz shout before I saw him standing behind her. "What in the hell are you doing, Marianne?" He was enraged.

My mother's voice no longer sounded like my mother when she shouted, "Get out of here! Get out, now!"

He yelled back, "You've lost your mind! I'll have no part of this madness! I'm calling the police. Get her out of there and clean her up!"

Somehow he convinced her and together then wrestled me from the bathtub. I looked back just before they dragged me through the door and saw the tub filled with blood. Blood spattered the wall and pooled on the floor where I had stepped from the tub.

Heinz and Mother laid me in bed and Mother toweled off the blood then pulled my nightgown over my head and arms. She covered me with blankets.

I hadn't noticed that Heinz had left the room until he returned and said, "The police are on their way."

"You called the police?" She asked angrily.

He spit loudly, "She could die, Marianne!"

I rolled away from the arguing voices and laid in a fetal position, sobbing. More voices added to theirs and soon the police led my mother from the room. A soft, male voice soothed me. "Stay calm," he said. "You must remain calm."

He convinced me to roll over to face him. I did and he shone a light in my eyes. Holding each eyelid open he examined my eyes closely. "How do you feel?" he asked.

I simply shook my head, unable to speak. I realized this wasn't a police officer, but a medic of some sort. Two policemen watched from behind him though.

He reached down next to the bed and pulled up a syringe. "This is something to take the edge off," he said before injecting the needle into my arm.

One officer knelt beside him and said to me, "You're safe now. We'll take care of you. Everything will be all right soon. Just stay calm."

His voice was soothing and my eyelids were so very, very heavy.

When I awoke in a hospital bed, I didn't recall how I'd gotten there. A priest stood over me and smiled warmly when he saw my eyes open. He took my hand and gently squeezed it. I know enough about the Catholic religion to know his words; he was administering the last rights.

I shook my head indicating that I wasn't ready to die yet.

"Easy child, you're safe," he assured me. "You've been through quite a nightmare."

*This is no nightmare*, I thought.

Then, he asked, "Please, tell me, who did this to you?"

I was stunned! Didn't he know that my mother had done this to me? Then I remember her words, *don't tell anyone or I'll be arrested!*

I opened my mouth but couldn't find the words to tell him. My mind raced with Mother's warning about being arrested. The tears burned my cheeks, endless, flowing tears. I heard whimpering sounds and realized that I made them. I wanted to scream and bellow and protest loudly, but I couldn't find the strength.

Then, Peter's voice sounded, "Hey, darling. How do you feel?"

He stepped around the Priest and took my hand. He sat and then leaned in close. "I love you. I thought we'd lost you."

I smiled through the sobs. He always made me smile, even through this.

"I love you," I whispered softly.

A woman appeared at the end of the bed suddenly. I recognized her as Peter's sister who I had met on several occasions and just now remembered that she was a registered nurse. Her expression, the sorrow and dismay, told me that she knew what happened. I also knew that the baby was gone.

Over the coming days the devastation over losing the baby hung over me like a dark cloud. I never knew the sex of the baby. We were never able to hear its first cry, its first laugh, or see the infant take its first steps. For this, I will never forgive my mother.

To say that I was angry with my mother would be an understatement. Words cannot express my outrage for a woman who I had once trusted implicitly. My mother betrayed me and had murdered her grandchild.

She also put her daughter's life, my life, in jeopardy. It was a miracle that two lives weren't taken within a few seconds.

In looking back, I believe she was afraid that she would not only have to take care of her daughter, but raise a grandchild too. Undoubtedly she recalled the difficulty of raising children when she was young, vulnerable and hurting.

When my mother became angry, she toughened to the point that I feared her.

I mention this because too often, when we find our children are expecting at a young age, we panic and don't think rationally. Look at the big picture, the celebration of the new life we are to be blessed with. All the rest are just details that will be addressed. Never seek a long term solution to a short term problem.

If it hadn't been for my stepfather's involvement over his fear for me, I probably wouldn't be here today.

## Chapter 13

After a few days of recuperation, I visited the doctor for a D&C, to assess the damage. The doctor felt confident that with the proper care and much rest, I should fully recover.

Peter called Aunt Helen to inform her of the news. From their conversation I realized that he had called her during my stay in the hospital and had continuously kept her apprised of the events. Aunt Helen, of course, insisted that we come to Worcester to stay until the whole thing calmed down.

Unfortunately, most of my personal belongings were still at Mother's apartment. Peter and I soon made plans to retrieve the rest of my things with a police escort, of course. Peter's brother, Doug, came along with us. Doug was the "muscle" of the family, for lack of a better description, and with all that had happened to this point, we expected trouble.

Peter, Douglas and I approached the door with a police officer at our shoulder. Soon after Douglas knocked, Heinz opened the door holding an axe.

Startled, the four of us stepped back. Heinz suddenly realized the predicament; his face flushed and he stammered, "I-I'm fixing a piece of wood in the house. Please come in." He quickly stowed the axe and led us inside the apartment. All of us sighed heavily with relief and entered.

"Your mother is away," Heinz told us. "I expect her back shortly. It might be best if you gather your things quickly."

Peter, Douglas and I snatched all we could in just minutes and left the apartment. At the curb, we said goodbye to the officer and he stood by until we drove away.

After Douglas and Peter dropped me at the apartment and helped haul all of my worldly possessions inside, Doug left to drive back home.

I had just finished putting my things away when Peter returned before dinnertime. We loaded in the car and drove north to stay with Aunt Helen in Worcester.

Upon our arrival, Aunt Helen had prepared my room. Once I was settled in, the three of us drove to town to check Peter into an old hotel. The hotel was so old that the elevator was run by a pulley system. Peter pulled the chain to carry the elevator up to his floor. He was quite fascinated with the workings of it all.

Peter, Aunt Helen and I spent the first night in the room talking about what had happened and were all still astounded at my mother's behavior. Peter stayed nights at the old hotel to allow me to rest. During the day he stayed at Aunt Helen's and we sat and talked mostly. We didn't laugh much, but were still overcome with grief at the loss of the baby and my relationship with Mother.

On our third evening, while in the kitchen visiting, the doorbell rang. Helen answered the door to find my mother in a rage that Helen had hidden me from her.

Peter and I heard her from the kitchen and I asked Peter to leave through the back door lest we antagonize her further. He left quickly and quietly, and I'm certain worried to leave me in her presence again.

No sooner had he closed the back door when Mother stormed into the kitchen, scolding me for leaving with Peter. I had trouble making out her words through her anger but I gathered that she intended to have me arrested, that I was too young to be away from home with Peter.

Aunt Helen tried to calm her for a time but when Mother refused to listen she phoned the police. On the rare occasion when Mother paused to take a breath, I heard Aunt Helen explaining over the phone all about my mother and the situation.

A policeman soon arrived and stepped in front of my mother, holding her firmly by the shoulders. His presence seemed to set her back some and she suddenly quieted. The officer ordered her to report to the police department immediately. Mother left the house and I doubted she had any intention of driving to the local precinct.

Peter, who had remained just outside the back door and out of sight, returned to the house just after Mother left. The officer advised that we should all follow him to the station so the police chief could sort out this mess.

At around 8 P.M. the three of us and Mother stood in the office of the police chief. He gave us all a moment to tell our side of the story. The man had a stern nature and even Mother kept her voice to an acceptable volume. When we'd all said our piece, the chief thought for a long moment, and then said, "Mrs. Krankemann, when you leave the station, you'll find the train station two blocks to the north, and three blocks east. Board the next train out of Worcester. Though I cannot tell you where to go, I suggest you return to the City, let the police there deal with your drama. Don't let me see you in Worcester again."

When she left, we thanked the Police Chief for his time. Outside of his office, Peter and I stood at a window looking down onto the street. The fog had set in and a lone street light lit my mother as she walked slow and alone and then vanished into the foggy night. Oddly, I was saddened to see her so alone.

To avoid any further judgment about Peter and I being together, Aunt Helen assisted us over the next two days to marry in front of a Justice of the Peace. Peter and I had planned to marry in Massachusetts after all that had happened. He obtained the blood test and all the required information that we needed and had brought it to Aunt Helen. On the 23$^{rd}$ of September we "tied the knot" in a civil ceremony. Now, rather than return to live with Aunt Helen, I stayed with Peter in the old hotel with the antique elevator. Finally, I felt happy despite the recent events. We spent a weekend in the hotel and the days were some of the most peaceful and joyous that I remember.

Peter and I left Worcester in his car to drive back to Staten Island. But first we stopped at a small farm in Connecticut for our honeymoon. As it turned out, Peter's mother had a cousin and her best friend from youth who lived on a small farm with her and her husband, who also had a small manufacturing business on the property. Peter's mother had just happened to be visiting her during the same weekend we were going through our trauma in Worcester, so we decided to stop in and say "hello." They asked us to stay the night, which we did, and that was our honeymoon.

Since Peter had been off work for this entire time, we said goodbye to Major Helen Magoon, WAC. Yes, during all of the turmoil Aunt Helen had been promoted to the rank of Major some weeks earlier and I couldn't be happier for her.

Peter resumed college at Wagner and worked at the Prudential Steamship Lines where he had been employed since leaving the Air Force in 1959. I got a job at the U.S. Lines as well and we would travel to lower Manhattan every day via Ferry and for the first time in my life I felt at ease and somewhat secure.

When things settled in at our new apartment, Peter and I decided to still be married in a church to seal our marriage in the eyes of God and the Catholic Church.

Peter and I both agreed to ask family and friends not to tell my mother. We had no intentions of inviting her and she certainly wasn't welcome.

We wed in *St. Theresa's Church* on Staten Island on October 9, 1960. Peter's mother held our reception in her apartment after the wedding ceremony. Many of Peter's friends and family attended making the day a true celebration. Of course, I was a nervous wreck throughout for fear that Mother would appear to dampen the glorious occasion. She never came and I assume she was unaware of the wedding until afterward. I'm certain that when she did find out, she was livid.

Wedding guests delivered a trove of gifts. Our simple apartment was furnished with little more than a mattress. The mattress surrounded by the many wedding presents made for an inspirational sight. Peter and I agreed that marrying twice must mean that we are destined to stay together until death do us part.

I was saddened that the situation with my mother couldn't somehow have been different. Every girl's dream is to be married with her mother in attendance, carrying on the family legacy. I know that one day, when I have a daughter of my own, that Peter and I will support her completely. We wouldn't dream of doing anything to put a dark cloud over her special day.

For Peter and me, life grew in wondrous ways. Peter enjoyed school and his employment. We made many new friends. Our tiny apartment soon became a cozy home. We enjoyed life on Staten Island and all the island had to offer.

A year and half later, I again became pregnant. Peter and I were overjoyed and set about making plans for the baby.

About two years after the wedding, approximately September of 1961, I received a telegram from my mother that read; *I've been having bad dreams. Please call.* She had included her phone number, the same phone number that she'd had since first renting her New York apartment.

I suppose by now that she had made peace with being unwelcome at our wedding. I suspected that word may have reached her that we were expecting a baby.

After discussing the telegram with both Peter and Aunt Helen, we decided a phone call couldn't hurt. When I phoned, I was surprised that Mother never apologized and she never mentioned the incident. Still, we talked at length about her life. I did get the sense however, that she wanted very much to be a part of our new family. She was still together with Heinz and had a surprise she wanted to tell me about. She and Heinz planned to marry and she wanted us both to attend. It had been two years since we had had our problems with her and had no contact at all, nor did we want any.

Heinz continued to work as a waiter at *The Bavarian Inn* and had taken time away from work to fly his wife to Cologne, Germany. Her request had been to die there and she had. Heinz had always impressed me as a hard worker, a dedicated husband, despite Mother's interference. Heinz had also been born and raised in Cologne and I imagine the time in his homeland had given him time to reflect. Mother said that sadly, Heinz and his wife had been married barely five years when she had developed the bone marrow cancer.

I suppose the conversation helped me appreciate Peter and our blessed marriage even more. He meant so much to me and was my best friend through the good times and my rock when life seemed unbearable.

I suppose our humanity lies in the ability to forgive those we love regardless of the circumstances. Mother re-entered our lives slowly, step-by-step and things went smoothly.

During the next few months we all prepared for the birth of our first child. I don't know for certain what Mother preferred as to the baby's sex, but for Peter and I, as long as the baby was born happy and healthy, we would embrace the blessing.

Mother visited often since she and Heinz had purchased a delicatessen on Dyckman Street in Upper Manhattan near their apartment. Mother and Heinz stayed busy running the Deli through the day and late into the night and throughout weekends. They worked hard and served good food. Heinz was a chef by profession, something I hadn't known before, and he was quite talented.

Mother was also a good cook, when she wanted to cook. Folks drove in all the way from New Jersey to buy their German potato salad and other authentic German food. In this new land, German's valued a little taste of home and paid well to obtain it.

Heinz and my mother soon married and held a small reception at the Hawaiian Room in the Lexington Hotel in downtown New York City in October of 1961.

Oma and Opa wedding day. October 1961
From left: Oma, Opa, Chrisel and Peter.

Peter and I attended of course. I felt relieved that she had decided to marry Heinz; he was a very good and kind person. When Heinz and Mother stood in front of the Justice of the Peace, Mother was nervous and fidgeted. I dreaded that she would change her mind. I liked Heinz. He was good for her and kept her somewhat settled.

**HOFMANN'S DELICATESSEN (1972)
64 SHERMAN AVE, NEW YORK**

Even after the wedding, Mother continued to be erratic. I never knew what she might say or do from one moment to the next. Somehow, I think Heinz found this endearing. He was the only person who could control her to some extent. When it got too much for him, he sometimes told her to be quiet or to "shut up." At the wedding he sensed her nervousness and calmed her by saying simply, "Let's do this."

Thank goodness she listened. The wedding went off without a hitch and everyone had a good time. Mother took the name Hofmann as her last name, now making her Marianne Jerke Hofmann.

We so wanted the baby to be delivered on Friday so Peter could be with me in the event that my hospital stay extended over the weekend.

Mother, Peter and I were home when the labor pains began. These pains were different than the others I'd experienced and soon were spaced close together. I told Peter that we'd better head for the hospital. Mother chimed in, "Hold on, I'm hungry. Wait while I fix a sandwich."

Peter grabbed the small suitcase that I'd packed ahead of time and passed by the kitchen where Mother dawdled to fix the sandwich.

"You come now, or you don't come at all," he told her gruffly.

I'm uncertain how she finished making that sandwich so quickly as she had the sandwich in one hand and her purse in the other when we all climbed into the car. In hindsight, I realize now that she likely knew how long a delivery could take for the first child. I lay in labor for twenty-four hours after the pains began. Heinz closed the deli and joined us at the hospital.

Our son, George, was born on February 11, 1962, two days after Peter's birthday.

Now we faced a dilemma, who would drive Oma and Opa, (which is grandma and grandpa in German) back to the ferry terminal?

After making some phone calls, Peter found that his Aunt Vivienne was free and available to drive them. Everyone liked Vivienne.

I had but one concern with her driving them to the ferry; Vivienne was a terrible driver. Case in point, after she'd picked up Oma and Opa from the hospital, she drove safely to the terminal, then drove over, or at least attempted to drive over a cement island that separated the cars lined up to board the ferry. The car high-centered on the cement blocks with Oma and Opa stuck in the car. Mother and Heinz were so shook up that they got out of car and walked quickly to the ferry leaving Vivienne alone in the car. The two of them leaving her like that didn't sit well with the rest of the family but I found the humor in it. I could just picture my mother storming out of the car and walking very fast with Heinz trailing after her.

A few days after the birth, Peter and I brought George home to our small apartment on Grimes Hill. I enjoyed playing house with our new son in the crib next to me.

One night when George was barely a week old, I heard an odd, creaking sound. A mother listens very carefully to every sound even when she sleeps. Mothers are even more alert with a newborn in the house. It was such a night when the moon shone directly into the room. The room was quite bright and when I opened my eyes I saw a lurking figure looking directly at our bed. I saw the man clearly but was so shocked that I could not even say the word "Peter". I took about a minute to call his name, I suppose.

Marianne and Christel with George after reconciliaion in 1962

"Peter! Peter!" I said sharply.

Peter sprang from bed immediately and ran after the man who made a hasty retreat through the open hallway door.

Peter, who was nearly naked, chased the man outside and down the street. I was shaken. Here had been a man with nerve enough to invade our apartment and bedroom, what might he do to Peter if Peter caught him?

It seemed like forever before Peter returned. We immediately called the police who arrived shortly and we filled out a report. Peter knew that I was so deeply disturbed by the incident that he rented us another larger apartment the following day. We moved out that very afternoon and evening.

About two weeks later little George, Peter and I drove toward Oma and Opa's new deli. We drove along the East River Drive to Dyckman street which is an interesting drive paralleling the East River. During a section of the drive, tugboats and small tankers sail along the

East River.

Destiny sometimes works wonders and today was just such a day. While we drove along, Capt. Douglas Hoverkamp piloted his ship in our direction of travel. We recognized the ship and actually saw him on deck. Peter and I called out from the car and he heard us and called back. Douglas yelled out and said, "I'll phone you when I get home from this trip!" When we eventually arrived at the deli, we were excited to tell Oma and Opa about seeing Douglas on the ship.

Over the years we were busy with family affairs, having more children, as well as working to make ends meet. Christopher followed George into our family on April 25, 1963.

After Christopher's birth, things settled down providing us with a peaceful, normal life for a few years.

1965, Hoffman Delicatessan
Oma and Opa with two staff members.

Peter and I often drove the boys to the deli to see Oma. We sometimes stopped along the way and bought flowers for Mother. When we arrived at the deli, Oma was always delighted with the flowers.

On each visit, Oma took each boy by the hand, provided them a brown paper shopping bag and they shopped in the deli, picking out whatever they wanted. All three of them delighted in this game.

One late afternoon in 1966 after visiting Oma when the boys were three and four years old, we drove toward home on Dyckman Street to Harlem River Drive. A great deal of social unrest and violence had recently been occurring in the Harlem area of New York. Along the right side of the highway, a bicycle path ran perpendicular to the highway and then ran right along the highway shoulder. From the corner of my eye I spied a girl on a bicycle coming down the path toward the highway. Two other children pushed her and she approached the parallel path turn too quickly to make the turn.

I screamed when she rode straight onto the highway in front of our car. Peter slammed on the brakes but it was too late.

The girl flew ten feet in the air and landed on the pavement in a heap. I immediately thought, *My god, she's dead!*

Peter's face was as pale as snow and I cried. I was horrified for the girl and for my boys having to see this. A moment later we gathered our wits and Peter and I jumped out of the car and ran to the girl.

"Don't touch her," Peter said. "We don't want to hurt her any worse."

I realized we were in Harlem and lately Harlem had frequently broken out with angry demonstrating crowds and even riots. Within minutes, a crowd of African Americans surrounded us. We were the only white people in sight and the mood was tense. I was horrified and I imagined Peter was too.

More people gathered quickly. I looked around terrified but I was more concerned for this girl than for my own safety. Besides, where could we run? A man stepped through the crowd. By his demeanor, the others knew him and he was a man of some authority. Soon, he quickly explained that he was an undercover policeman.

The officer knelt beside the girl and felt her neck for a pulse. He bent over and put his ear close to her mouth. "She's breathing," he said quietly.

"Do you think she'll be all right?" I asked and my voice squeaked with nervousness.

"She's unconscious, I expect she'll come around soon." He stood up and asked us to leave and drive on; I was grateful as the crowd made me very nervous.

"An ambulance is on the way," the officer told me. "It would be best if you two get into your car, lock the doors and drive straight home."

Peter shook his head and said, "I don't feel good leaving her like this."

The officer looked him squarely in the eyes. "I'll take care of it. The best thing you can do to keep everything calm is to drive away. The sooner you do that, the safer we will all be. Please," he motioned toward our car with his head, "go."

Once in the car, of course we had difficulty remaining calm while attempting to drive home. I'm glad Peter drove; my hands were shaking too badly. Soon after we arrived home, Peter called our insurance company and advised them of the accident.

I slept little that night, as did Peter, I'm sure. Since I'm a mother and this child of course had a mother, I felt a strong need to see this little girl and to know that she had survived. The following morning after Peter drove off to work, I left the house and made my way to the subway. I boarded the train and rode deep into Harlem, never once questioning my judgment.

I knew where to find the hospital nearest to the accident since we had often driven through Harlem. I got off the subway at a stop nearest the hospital and climbed the concrete steps to the street. After I walked no more than a block or so, I heard a ruckus coming from the next block over. Smoke rose above the buildings. People were shouting in the distance and glass broke. Police sirens sounded steadily. I quickened my pace.

When I entered the hospital, a nurse greeted me.

"Hi," I said nervously. "Yesterday, my husband I were driving through the area and our car struck a little girl. Is she here?"

A tall, black man approached us and asked, "Are you here to see the little girl on the bicycle?"

When I told him that I was, his eyes flamed and he raised his hand. I stepped back suddenly to avoid a strike.

Then, he stopped and asked angrily, "What is that accent you speak with? Where are you from?"

My heart raced. This man scared me badly. The nurse stepped in between us and said to me, "I'll take you to see the girl." She glared at the man sternly, and asked him, "Why don't you get some coffee?"

We turned away from the man and entered the hallway. I didn't dare look back to see if he had left.

The nurse said, "That's her father, but you've probably figured that out."

"Yes, I'm so sorry."

"You see, about a year ago, someone doused his son in gasoline and lit him on fire. His son suffered terribly before he passed away. He hasn't been right in the head since then."

My stomach ached. A lump formed in my throat but I managed to choke out, "That poor, poor man."

She placed her hand on my back and guided me inside of a room. The lights were dim and the only sound came from the steady beep of machines.

The little girl looked up from a bed near the window to see us. I imagined her to be about ten-years old, older than my sons. Her eyes were clear behind the scraped cheeks and forehead. Plaster casts covered both of her legs and her right arm was heavily bandaged. My heart ached for this poor broken child.

"Hi there," I said quietly.

She nodded, uncertain what to say.

"I was in the car yesterday when we hit you." The words seemed empty and yet so tragic.

"Oh," she said softly.

"My name is Christel and I have two little boys. I've been worried sick about you all night. How do you feel?"

"It hurts mostly," she said.

The nurse stepped out of the room, leaving us alone. I sat at the edge of her bed.

"I'm so sorry," I told her. "We just didn't see you coming."

It took some time for her to warm up to me. When she realized that I had come to see her because I genuinely cared about her, she talked more freely. After we had talked for some time, I thought I had better head home before her father returned. I asked, "I'd like to buy you a gift before I go. What would you like?"

The girl shrugged.

"Come on, you can tell me. Anything you'd like."

Then she whispered as though revealing a secret, "I'd like a doll."

I smiled and squeezed her one hand that wasn't bandaged. "A doll it is. I'll be back shortly."

I left her there and walked the hallway toward the door where I'd come in. I felt more sorrow than I had in years over this little injured girl so full of life and filled with forgiveness. What a wonder, she was. Filled with mixed emotions I was sick for her, of course, and tremendously relieved that she would eventually heal.

I left the hospital and looked up the street both ways. About a block away I spotted a store that looked as though it might carry a doll.

The noise from the next block had quieted some, though I heard what I thought were two gunshots followed by more police sirens. I soon entered the store and browsed the shelves toward the rear. The cashier and another store worker were black, of course, as were all of the shoppers. Such a different world from mine! Although everyone inside seemed more interested in their business than mine, I still felt uncomfortable.

I spotted the doll that I imagined would bring a smile to the little girl's face and tucked it under one arm. I paid at the front register and left to return to the hospital.

When I handed over the gift, she showed me a bright smile. "Thank you," she said, politely. Regardless of my first impression of her father, apparently the man had raised her right.

She held the doll to her chest and I asked that she let the doll take care of her. She nodded to me and then waved when I left the room.

I walked quickly back to the subway and boarded, anxious to return home to my family. I never heard from the little girl again, nor did we ever hear anything about a lawsuit or even a traffic ticket.

In March of 1968, I neared the end of another pregnancy, this time a girl who we had decided to name Heidi. We rented a house with a separate garage on Willowbrook Road on Staten Island.

Our physician, Dr. Gianvito had delivered both boys on Staten Island and he would deliver our daughter as well. Days before giving birth, the boys contracted chickenpox. We didn't want to risk germs in the house with a newborn on the way so Mother arranged to have them visit her place in New York and she would care for them.

Peter drove the boys over to Oma and she took good care of

them until they recovered from the chickenpox. After the boys had left, Peter's brother's wife came to Staten Island from New Jersey to clean and disinfect the house so that Dr. Gianvito wouldn't object to the baby coming home when she was ready.

Three months later, the time arrived for the baby to be born. I had taken a job teaching honor students in a private school. To hide my pregnancy I sat each day when the students entered the classroom and remained seated until after they had left. I truly enjoyed teaching and taught right up until my delivery day.

Heidi was born on March 18, 1968 and we took her home two days after the birth. Mother had returned the boys home and our family was reunited.

## Chapter 14

Mother and Heinz owned the delicatessen for a number of years. They did well in the business, but of course a deli is a lot of work. Mother isn't one to settle into quiet routine for long. Everything must always be done her way. She began to organize rallies and raised money for Christmas ornaments to decorate the streets. She collected money from various stores in the neighborhood, from the bakeries, laundries and hardware stores mostly.

Then, one day, the streets were decorated with wreaths on streetlamps and the city had accommodated her by filling in the potholes. Where shady characters once loitered in the streets, shoppers wandered the streets and shopped in the stores. The less desirable characters moved on to other neighborhoods.

Mother instituted change. When folks needed help, they called my mother day or night. She worked closely with the police department to help the needy. They were her neighbors and she took her responsibility seriously.

When cars blasted loud music, Marianne went to the car door, opened it and demanded that they turn it down. I was certain that one day someone would hurt her. I saw her often in the middle of the street during a traffic jam, directing traffic.

At home in her apartment building she organized the tenants to hold their rent payments until the landlord fixed whatever was broken, or even until he made changes to install better windows or lighting in the cellar. She worked with the landlord to install speakers at the front door. People now had to "buzz in" and each resident knew who they were letting in.

She began a campaign to catch thieves and to help the New York City 34th Precinct. Marianne Hofmann readily helped the police on the streets. The elderly who had trouble could call her and tell her what they saw on the streets or in the buildings. Heinz never wanted a part of this business; he kept busy enough with the delicatessen.

She amazed us with her energy when helping others. She enjoyed staying busy and involved. Marianne organized church rallies and she helped an untold number of young students. If someone saw anyone bully a child, they came to her and she did something about it right away. Soon, everyone knew her.

While my mother was so busy, Peter had graduated from *Wagner College* on Staten Island, December 1965 and began working for Mobil Corporation on April 25, 1966.

With the new job, Peter and I moved to a different town every two years. He received promotions and advanced well with Mobil Oil. We lived in New York from 1966 to 1968; Boston until 1970, then to Scarsdale until 1974. When he worked in the Mobil Headquarters in New York City, we moved to New Jersey until 1976.

In 1976 Peter received a job transfer to London, England. Of course Mother didn't like us moving such a long way from home. England is a long way to visit.

Peter had an upcoming meeting that required him to fly to California and he asked if I could go with him. Of course, I wanted to go, but we had no one to watch the children, so I asked Mother to watch them, with one stipulation, don't take them to the nudist camp! Since Florida was now in a severe winter with extreme cold weather, I thought she just might be able to pull this off.

Peter and I left for California and had a wonderful time, his meetings went well and we were able to spend time together sightseeing. We ate out every night, stayed in a fine hotel and the time, for me at least, was very relaxing. I called home just two days before we were scheduled to fly back and all seemed well when I spoke with Mother, until Heidi got on the phone.

"Oma and Opa took us to the camp!" She nearly squealed into the phone.

My face flushed, I bit into my lip hard to keep from screaming.

Heidi went on, "Some people were playing tennis and the only clothing they had were socks and shoes!"

I let her go on until she had finished. I don't recall the rest of her conversation I was so angry. Heidi put the boys on the phone, George and Christopher, and both told me they had had a lot of fun with Opa and Oma.

When we returned, Peter and I picked up the children and took them home. Peter had cautioned me not to speak, that if I did, who knows what the consequences might be. It was many months before I had calmed down enough to invite Heinz and Mother to the house again.

Shortly before our scheduled departure Peter's brother, Fred, gave us a farewell shindig at their house. It was a large family gathering. Opa was the chef and Oma provided all of the conversations. "Do this and do that," "bring this and bring that" is all that we heard. She still hadn't adjusted to our leaving.

When the limo finally arrived to pick us up I was mildly surprised. Mobil Oil, in the past, had always provided a shiny limousine with a driver who dressed the part. This driver wore cowboy boots and hat and the limo was sub-par.

We said goodbye to Heinz, Mother and the rest of the family.

Mother at least managed to say, "Goodbye, bon voyage, and make sure you write and call me when you get there."

Our little family stepped into the limo and off we went. After a short limousine ride that went off without a hitch, we arrived at the New York International Airport. Our next stop would be London, England, which promised a new life, a new school for the children and a new job for Peter. I looked forward to a new home.

Weeks after arriving in London, Peter and I moved into a house in Woking Surrey, England. Woking lies outside of London, Peter had to take a train into London for work. We were lucky that it was an express train stop, but I had to drive him to the train station every day unless he traveled. The house had been dubbed "Tanah Kita," which is Indonesian for "our country." The house was surrounded completely by rose gardens in our yard and in the neighbor's yard; giving it a unique and homey feel.

While we adjusted to life in England, Mother continued helping the New York police and worked hard to institute a form of rent control. She kept so busy trying to clean up New York City that crime rate did lower. Marianne Hofmann had made a big difference in her neighborhood community.

We learned that London is one of the most civilized cities in the world. London boasts many museums, with a wealth of history to keep an entire family occupied. With exhibitions, castles, you name it you will find everything to entertain a family.

On one particular day we had arranged to attend a show. The children stayed home and we all dressed up in time to arrive at the London show early. While waiting at the show house for our friends to arrive, Peter sat next to me reading a newspaper. Peter had developed a fascination with newspapers. He always needed to be current on events, to know what was going on, and what's new in town and throughout the world. I sat enjoying all the well-dressed men and the beautiful ladies arriving wearing their finest clothes. When our friends arrived and sat next to us, Peter suddenly smashed the newspaper into his lap, like he does sometimes when he's upset or excited about something.

He turned to me and he said, "Christel, your mother has done it again."

*New York Times article for Marianne's Law and Order rally.*

I asked, "What do you mean?" He handed me the paper and I read an article, quite a long one, about my mother. I couldn't believe what I read. Here we are in London; I'm dressed in an evening gown and Peter in a tuxedo. The newspaper article told of Marianne Hofmann who had rented Madison Square Garden for one night to hold a rally to clean up New York City. The rally was directed toward the media and city officials and anyone else interested in cleaning up the City. According to the report, she had borrowed six-thousand dollars from a bank. She had committed to lowering violence in New York City and to help the police department in their valiant efforts. The article also mentioned that her husband, Heinz Hofmann, had absolutely no idea what she intended for the night.

Of course, Madison Square Garden is very large and she had rented *The Felt Forum* calling for greater police protection in the city. Fewer than one-thousand people had attended but the publicity was overwhelming.

The article continued, "Mrs. Hofmann strongly argues that one cannot blame the police for all of these problems in the community; she blames the politicians. The police can only do so much, especially when they are on call and working on their particular jobs. She said, 'the politicians need to change. They give a speech and then another speech and so on and nothing gets done. When politicians promise something, they should be made to fulfill those promises. Year after year they make the same promises'."

The paper clearly showed her anger and concern and even stated that "Hofmann's spirit never flags." And I'm honored to read Mother say, "I gave my daughter this advice, when she turned fourteen, 'always smile, be polite and respect others. But when you promise something, even if it hurts, you must do it."

It had been some time since I'd been proud of my mother, and now, I had good reason to be.

Over the years, Mother had taught me the value of being connected to the police when you live in the neighborhood. She felt that citizens need to show more enthusiasm and take charge in keeping their neighborhoods free of violence and crime. She thought neighbors should be respectful of others, including the police and politicians. And when people ask for help from the police and politicians or the neighbors, they should receive immediate help. She believed in building clinics with councils and advocates for people who are concerned about the community's problems, with drugs, robberies, trouble parking and illegal peddling. And she believed in establishing the clinics first, above anything else.

Scores of people, including the sick, the elderly and handicapped should be helped as a priority. Many crimes stem from those who don't have the money to help their family when they are sick or poor. They need small banks to help the people rather than the large banks helping themselves first. And according to the article, these are the things she intended to address at the rally and in the months to come.

I asked Peter, "Can you believe this newspaper article? She

reaches out to us even when we are across the ocean in a British theater in London, England."

Later, I called my mother but I talked to Heinz instead; he said he didn't want to know anything. I can only assume that his wife's time away from the delicatessen had been a source of contention between them.

Peter's mother, Audrey Smith, and Aunt Vivienne Kuhrt came to visit in Woking Surrey, England. While there, they asked to visit Brighton after having heard that it was quite beautiful. I made the hotel arrangements, gave them the name and the address and drove them to the train station. When they arrived in Brighton, they hailed a taxi and provided the driver with the name and address. The cab driver turned in his seat and said, "You should not want to go there. This is no longer a hotel; it's been turned into a brothel in an undesirable section of the city.

"Oh my goodness!" Aunt Vivienne exclaimed. "Can you please suggest a much better hotel that is safe and beautiful on the Brighton coast?"

The driver simply smiled, shifted gears and told them, "I know just the place."

True to his word, the cabbie drove them to a beautiful hotel right on the Brighton coast. They enjoyed their stay, often walking the beach in the morning and evening. Brighton is close enough to Woking that we were able to drive down to visit during their stay.

When their grandmother and Aunt Vivienne returned to London, our children gave them the grand tour of Woking. They took Vivienne to the tennis courts since she liked to play tennis. The children then took them to Cobham and showed them the American School.

Some-time after grandma and Aunt Vivienne returned to the States, my mother came to visit. She enjoyed her stay. We attended a London show, toured the Tower of London, several museums and she especially enjoyed the double-decker buses. She loved the pubs and the bobbies, (policemen), but twice she was nearly killed trying to cross the street. The cars in England drive on the opposite side of the lane than they drive in the States. She had difficulty remembering this. Thankfully she arrived home safely and without further incident.

I had known that for many years Mother had been corresponding with Maria Loeckher, Marga's mother, in Fuessen, Germany. We talked about that during her visit. She believed that Maria and her family knew more about our family's history than we did! Mother had written her for nearly twenty-five years now and I admired her dedication.

Peter had received word that he was to transfer to Indonesia in the coming months. With time in England coming to a close, Peter arranged for Mother and I to return to Germany to visit. Mother told me that Marga was now married and had had two daughters.

Her husband's name was Arthur. Ulla was her oldest daughter and Claudia their younger girl.

Mother and I packed and within days we drove to Heathrow Airport and flew to Munich, Germany.

The flight from Heathrow was pleasant and oddly, rather an empty flight. In Munich we rented a car and I drove to Bavaria via the "Romantic road" which is a very scenic route. We chose a route that took us through the beautiful mountains and forests.

When we arrived in Fuessen, we parked the car in front of Marga's front door. The amazing thing was that when Marga stepped out the front door she was a blonde, where she had always had brown hair before. And when I stepped out of the car, I had also dyed my hair blonde. From that moment when we saw each other, the twenty-five years separating us just melted away. We had never lost our friendship and we had never even known it was still with us.

It seemed to be the same for Marianne and Maria. We unpacked our bags in the apartment and then sat over coffee, relaxing and catching up with the latest news.

It seemed that we sat and talked for days. Mother and I shared a bedroom. Maria and Marianne laughed and even cried at times. The visit was wonderful and I know Mother delighted in being back in Fuessen.

The following day, Marga and I left Maria and Mother home while we walked through town. This was our time to share the special words that only best friends can share. To me, this was like having a sister again. She was still beautiful and gracious, just as she had always been.

Each evening we went out on the town to meet with friends from school. Marga had kept in touch with many that we knew and it was so good to see them all again.

Mother and Maria spent most of their time at the apartment just talking. One night we decided to go out and Marga took us to *Kobel Alm*, a place similar to a discotheque but more like a Bavarian pub. Shortly after we arrived, I noticed that her oldest brother, Paul, was in the pub seated with a friend in a corner. Both were drinking quite a lot of beer. The pub owner stopped by on a few occasions to chat with him and something seemed amiss. Paul seemed intent on drowning himself in a large mug of German Beer.

I left Marga at the table and went to their table to see what was wrong. Paul introduced me to his friend, Herman and we exchanged pleasantries for a few minutes.

Though I could tell that Paul wanted to talk to me, he found it difficult to say what he wanted. Finally, I asked straight up, "What is bothering you?"

Paul's eyes watered, then a tear trickled down each cheek.

"My mother is very ill," he told me while Herman listened in though I sensed that Herman already knew the story. "She's been diagnosed with A.L.S." (Lou Gherig's disease.)

My heart nearly stopped. *Maria?* I thought. *No...*

He must have read the disbelief in my eyes because he nodded slowly and wiped his eyes.

"I just found out today," he said. "Mother couldn't even tell me, she asked the doctor to talk with me."

I now realized that my mouth hung open. I closed it and covered my lips with my fingers.

"Things will be tough for her," he added, and then gulped from the beer mug.

"What is A.L.S.?" I asked. Although I had heard of the sickness, I didn't know the details, nor did I completely know if I wanted to know.

"A.L.S. attacks the nervous system. It breaks down the control of the muscles. A person gets weaker, can suffer spasms, and even have trouble talking, swallowing and even breathing."

Stunned as I was, I attempted to console him. "Your mother is one of the strongest women I know. I sat close and held his hand. He wouldn't meet my eyes, he just drank. "Paul, you'll get a handle on this. You need to get it together and be strong for her, okay?"

He muttered something unintelligible and I realized the alcohol was affecting him worse than I'd initially realized. "We'll talk later," I told him before leaving the table.

When I returned and sat at our table, Marga knew from my expression that Paul had told me about her mother. She began to tear up. I slid my chair close to her and put my arm around her. "I think we'd better get out of here," I said.

She nodded and we stood up, gathered our purses and made our way toward the door. She signaled to Paul to follow when we passed his table. Paul staggered out behind us and into the street.

While Paul did his best to keep up, Marga and I wandered the brick streets and talked. She told me what she knew, which included few more details than what Paul had provided.

As we walked, I realized that I still hadn't grasped that Maria was so sick. She seemed full of life, enjoyed everyone, especially seeing Mother again. I supposed that destiny had brought us to Fuessen, to be with our dear friends at such a difficult time.

We arrived home safely but Paul was clearly drunk. He swaggered into my bedroom and fell onto the bed. I don't know if he had forgotten that I was staying in his room, and that my mother was asleep in the next bed, or if he could even think clearly.

"Get up!" I whispered. "You go upstairs. My mother's asleep and so is yours." I tugged on his arm, trying to pull him from the bed.

Paul has a large frame and stands six foot, four inches tall; a man who is clearly too big for me to move alone.

I stepped into the hallway and called quietly upstairs, "Marga..."

Marga appeared at the top of the stairs with a cocked eyebrow.

"Paul is in my bed!" I said, quietly.

She laughed, "he what?"

"He's in my bed and I can't get him up! I'm afraid he'll wake my mother."

Marga didn't lose the smile as she navigated the stairs and followed into my bedroom. We both grabbed his arms and helped him toward the stairs.

The semi-conscious Paul tried to assist as much as he could; stumbling while managing the stairs. We finally half-dragged him upstairs and into his room. Marga and I were both spent when we dropped him in bed and we parted ways for our bedrooms and a good night's sleep.

The following day, the household ran as normal so as not to upset Maria. I was curious to know if Maria had told my mother.

Mother and I visited the convent school in Geimersheim. I was curious to see if any of the nuns who had taught while I was there, were still there. To my pleasant surprise, Schwester Marianne was one of the first to greet us. The year before my husband and three children had visited the school with me and I actually saw Schwester Marianne then. Now I was back with just my mother and our visit was cordial.

We stayed with Marga and the family for another two days then

1977 - Christel and children with her favorite teacher; Schwester Marianne

packed up to leave again. Saying goodbye was more difficult than I could have ever imagined. The entire family gathered at the apartment before we left for the airport. We sat for two hours and shed a lot of tears before Mother and I finally climbed in the car and steered toward the Munich airport.

Hours later, Mother and I arrived in Woking England. We unpacked and while we prepared for her flight back to New York in just two days, one question weighed on my mind.

As we sat over a cup of coffee the night before her flight out, I asked, "Did you enjoy seeing Maria?"

Her face fell somber. "Yes, I did."

"I didn't get as much chance to see her as I'd have liked. How is she?"

Mother sensed what I alluded to. Her eyes watered and she sipped from her cup. Then, she said, "Not long before we left, she confided in me. She's sick, quite sick."

I only nodded in response.

"Her doctor diagnosed her with Lou Gehrig's disease."

"Yes," I whispered reverently.

Oma (Marianne) with two sisters who still knew Christel from the convent school.
1978

I realized then that Mother's visit with Maria had affected her more than I had known. Mother never saw Maria again as the Lou Gherig's disease took the best of Marga's mother and she passed a few years later.

As I grow older, I've come to know that often when we reconnect with longtime friends, we expect to see them just as we remember them. We expect that we both are somehow immune to aging though their eyes and faces reflect our own battle scars.

# Chapter 15

Peter was transferred in 1978 to Jakarta, Indonesia. We packed up the family from our wonderful Woking home and traveled to Indonesia.

We arrived, rented a home this time and settled in quickly. Peter and I had moved so often that we had learned shortcuts to settling in. We unpacked all the essential boxes first, and then spent one long day unloading and unpacking everything else. Once everything was put away, we began to settle into our home quickly.

After we were there a year or so my mother wanted to come for a visit. We made all the arrangements.

On this trip, Marianne Hofmann nearly created an international incident. Her ticket was from New York to Hong Kong-then from Hong Kong to Jakarta. On the plane she talked with two men that were sitting next to her. While they talked, she found out that they were staying at the same hotel in Hong Kong. The three intended to meet later at the hotel and then go sightseeing, which they did.

Unfortunately Marianne forgot to return to the hotel and pack up in time to make her next flight out. Knowing that she needed to check out at the front desk she packed everything, including the small bottles in the room's minibar refrigerator. She placed them carefully into her oversized purse and hauled her luggage to the front desk. At the desk, the clerk asked her to pay for the small alcohol bottles. Mother was adamant that she thought the bottles were free and she certainly wouldn't pay for them. Realizing the stalemate, she removed the bottles from her purse and lined them all on the desk in front of her.

During the fiasco, which took longer than she intended, she had missed her flight out.

Christel and Heidi attending a traditional Indonesian wedding.

In the cab on the drive to the airport, she became so frustrated that she began to cry. Mother didn't often get upset enough to cry. She realized that her daughter and her family would be waiting at the airport. She had already said goodbye to the two men and she had no idea what to do now.

After arriving at the airport, she washed the tears from her face in the public restroom and then stood in line at the ticket counter. Once she arrived at the counter, she explained her situation and asked for help. The ticket agent was sympathetic with this lady who was on the verge of tears. She booked her on the next flight, first-class.

At the Jakarta airport, we waited for the plane that she had been booked on to empty. When all passengers had exited, Oma hadn't appeared.

I went to the airline desk while Peter waited with the children and I asked them what had happened to Marianne Hofmann, my mother. I asked how they could possibly miss an elderly lady who was registered on that flight.

The airline hadn't realized that she hadn't boarded. They had no notice that a sixty-two year old grandmother was missing.

Needless to say, I was upset. I threatened to call the American Embassy and tell them about this situation. Finally after some frantic searching on their computer, the agent said she was on the next plane. We thanked him and left for the gate but were still quite anxious. At the time, we didn't know that it hadn't been the fault of the airline.

After she arrived and we had said our anxious 'hello's' and exchanged our hugs, we asked her what the heck had happened? Mother matter-of-factly told us that she had been having too much fun sightseeing and had made a mistake.

I was incensed! "Didn't you know how worried we would all be? What were you thinking, Mother? That was terribly irresponsible!"

This time she almost apologized, in her own way. She thanked us for worrying. Our excitement to see her overrode any ill feelings.

Indonesia is a wonderful and beautiful country and we all had a great time showing her Jakarta. We took her to the American School where she enjoyed the people. They were all so friendly and polite, as were most Indonesians. The Indonesians are also quite talented.

Mother enjoyed shopping because in Jakarta, at least, shoppers bargain with the vendors. This provided an added incentive to her, to not only haggle for the best price, but to get to know the seller as well. She left more than one of them laughing and they seemed to see her as a new American friend.

Mother stayed with us for a week. She arrived safely back in New York where Heinz picked her up at the airport.

Peter was transferred again in 1980 to Stavanger, Norway. Stavanger, the fourth most populated Norwegian city lies on the country's southwest corner and on the North Sea Coast. Surrounded by water, the metropolis never warms up like most inland cities do. The core of downtown consists mainly of eighteenth and nineteenth century wooden houses that the government protects from being torn down and replaced. This adds a unique old world charm that the residents cherish.

Norway is very different than anywhere we had lived, or even visited. The mountainous terrain is breathtaking and sometimes extremely cold. The waterfalls are powerful and amazing. Sun shines on the waterfalls producing beautiful rainbows. At times we experienced rains on one side of a bridge, and snow on the other side, this is how quickly the weather changes. This also makes the Norway roads dangerous to travel.

Oil and gas drilling are big business in the North Sea. Stavanger is the headquarters for Mobil Oil and was the center for the construction of the Statfjord (platform) Oil Fields that has now three Condeep Concrete Production Platforms A,B, and C. This is why Peter had been transferred. Stavanger is one of the most expensive cities to live in but a wonderful place, especially for expats like us.

The city is centered around the Stavanger Cathedral which had been built in the year 1125; the year the city claims that it was first founded.

This time, Peter made arrangements for Oma and Opa to come and visit us in Stavanger. It occurred to me that perhaps this time, with Heinz next her, she might just make the flight without incident.

However, as I've mentioned, my mother is unpredictable. Mother was excited to celebrate Christmas with Peter and me and more so with her grandchildren. She dearly loved the children.

The plane arrived as scheduled, but no Oma and Opa. We did notice the last passengers to exit however; a Santa Claus in full uniform stepped out followed shortly by Opa. After Santa went down the stairs, Opa followed with their bags.

Peter muttered softly, "Oh my, what has happened now? This does not look good." After another moment, he added, "what in the world has she done now?"

Heidi who stood next to me was becoming anxious. Her face flushed with embarrassment.

Seemingly from nowhere, newspaper reporters appeared from the crowd, one man mentioned that a woman had notified the papers that she had intended a surprise for her family who were waiting for her to celebrate the holidays.

She arrived in full costume with a guitar in hand as she sang Christmas carols. I overheard a flight attendant tell the plane's captain that this time the flight felt very Christmassy and that she enjoyed it immensely. The pilot smiled wide.

Heidi said to me, "Mom, I don't believe this..."

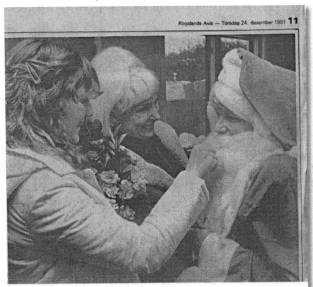

*Newspaper photo of Marianne's arrival as Santa at the Stavenger, Norway airport*

When Peter returned to work the following day, one of the men at the office mentioned the crazy woman on the plane that went to the restroom and emerged, dressed as Santa Clause. As she walked the aisle to her seat, she asked each passenger; "Did you behave yourself this year?" and she often added, "I wish you a very Merry Christmas," or "Ho, ho, ho! Merry Christmas to all!"

We found out later that Mother had notified every newspaper in the area after she had first checked with the flight's captain. He gave her his best wishes, mentioning "it will be different, maybe add some Christmas spirit to the flight."

Peter hadn't said a word to his coworker that this was his mother-in-law. Still, after a few days, someone in the office discovered his secret and I'm sure made his life unbearable for weeks.

We enjoyed a magical holiday season. Christmas in Norway is truly special since every Christmas is a white Christmas. The Norwegians celebrate traditionally in fine fashion. When Oma and Opa flew back to New York things settled down again for a while.

Our house was cozy and comfortable through the winters, despite the sunlight not reaching us so far north until after 10:30 A.M. The sun sets again about 4:30, which makes for long, cold nights. Summers were the opposite; all day the sun is strong with only a few hours of darkness, which makes sleeping difficult.

***

After three years in Stavanger, Norway, Mobile once again transferred Peter to Chicago, Illinois as part of a small management team to Container Corp. of America (CCA) to help manage business. CCA was a large pulp and paper manufacturer which Mobil had purchased a few years earlier and was struggling to remain profitable.

Each time we moved we had to sell our house in the States. We had settled in Hindsdale, Illinois for about half a year when Marga and three girls flew in from Germany to visit. Marga, the three girls and I packed into our car and drove together to vacation in the Florida sunshine.

The men had driven down earlier in Christopher's car because we wanted the cars in Florida to leave for later use.

During the early part of the trip, Marga tried to drive our big car. Previously, she had only been accustomed to the smaller German makes, which handled much differently than American made luxury cars. Getting used to the size of the vehicle was difficult for her and at one time, she pulled into a toll booth and pulled in so close that the spray from the windshield wipers showered the toll booth attendant.

Embarrassed, she pulled from the toll booth to the side of the highway and allowed me to drive the rest of the way.

We stopped at a Holiday Inn in Northern Alabama for the night. After settling into our rooms, we went down to the restaurant for dinner.

We ordered our meals from a pleasant young lady and we all sat talking while waiting for our meals.

A waiter approached the table with a full tray of food and I noticed the man sweated profusely and sweat was dripping on our food! I didn't know how they did things in the south, but this wasn't appropriate by my standards. I stood from the table and held out both hands, stopping him from placing any of the plates on our table.

In a stern, yet polite voice, I told him, "I don't mean to offend you, young man. You certainly appear to be working very hard, but you're sweating all over the food! Please take those plates back to the kitchen, wash up and bring us fresh food."

Of course he was embarrassed. Still, he lifted the tray of dinner plates and returned to the kitchen. We waited unusually long, but eventually he did return, freshened up and laid out what we had to assume were freshly made plates.

We continued the trip the following day and took a bit of a detour from the freeway when one of the girls began to have stomach pains, and then diarrhea. We pulled into a gas station in a little town named Intercourse, Alabama, which we found a rather bizarre name for a town.

Our friend went off to find the restroom in this peculiar little station while a young man pumped gas into the car. Marga and the girls went inside to shop for some snacks, leaving me standing outside the car with the young station attendant.

Strangely, he began mumbling while he pumped gas, strange mumblings of someone murdering his best friend. From the little I could interpret of his ramblings, the murder had happened just a day ago and he was afraid for his life.

I paid him for the gas and then ran inside. I collected Marga and the girls and we returned to the car in a rush and left that little town behind. Once out of town I told them what had happened and we all laughed and talked about that even long after our arrival in Winter Haven, Florida.

***

We had left Norway and we moved back to the States in 1983 for Chicago. Norway's climate was just too cold in winter, the days were too short and sunshine too infrequent. The Chicago house was beautiful, but the weather was so cold there too that Peter's parents couldn't go outside, despite being bundled up warm, and taking deep breaths. The cold air hurt their lungs. We spent only a year in Chicago.

In 1984 Peter's job took him to Saudi Arabia. This was to be a very different way of life for all of us. I figured it out that Peter in pressing further, he admitted that he was afraid to have her visit and the Saudis had not banned her from the country. Arabian women are subjected to strict laws and adherence to tradition, keeping their heads covered and sometimes faces covered, never speaking against a man, and others. Of course, I understood his viewpoint. Mother did eventually come to visit us in Saudi Arabia and handled the Arabian traditions wonderfully. What was most interesting was that Opa had been in this area much earlier and one day he told me his story.

Heinz was born in central Germany near Frankfurt in a small town named Niederweise-Hessen on 31 December 1920. He left home at the age of fourteen and signed onto a tramp steamer carrying coal to England where he performed duties as a steward's helper. For the next several years, he continued to sail in the German Merchant Marine as both steward and cook.

Opa was in the German merchant marine when the war began. His ship was in the Red Sea in about the year 1942 at a port on the African east coast. Opa told us that his ship was in a small convoy of three German ships that the British found in port. Before they could depart and outrun the British, their German officers thought they could serve the war better by joining up with the Italian army, an ally of the Germans, which at the time was in East Africa.

Sometime later the British captured them along with some Italians and sent them to an internment camp in South Africa.

Heinz remained in the South African camp for the remainder of the war. During his internment, he learned to speak Afrikansk, learned to survive in the desert and made some lifelong friends.

The severe desert heat and humidity made life almost unbearable.

He learned the importance of keeping perishable food cold. They buried food in a pit and then covered it with a drenched cloth then dripped water over the cloth to simulate a refrigerator.

When the war ended and he was released, Heinz made his way back to Cologne, Germany and found work in a restaurant called the *Cologne Bahnhof Station*.

He married and immigrated to the United States in the mid-1950's, as I mentioned earlier.

Heinz spoke five languages fluently; German, French, Africansk, Italian and English.

Opa introduced us to some of the friends he had made years ago in the camp who now lived in New York City.

George eventually married and in August of 1988, he and his wife, Kristy, gave birth to a baby boy, Asheton Hoverkamp. Our grandson was born at the *Regency Medical Center* in Winter Haven. Unfortunately, Asheton was born prematurely and required an incubator. Because the hospital was relatively new and still experienced some growing pains, the incubator was also faulty and the air stopped flowing to his little lungs. His lungs eventually collapsed putting him in grave danger. The nurse responded quickly and Kristy also realized what was happening. Fortunately, the infant experienced no permanent damage and we could chalk it up to a close call.

During the weeks that Kristy and George stayed at the hospital with the baby; Heinz cooked their meals and helped with the baby and whatever else they needed. Since we were stranded overseas, we were especially grateful for Opa in these weeks. Oddly, my mother never held the baby, nor Kelsey and other subsequent grandchildren. This was very different from Opa, who nearly insisted on holding them whenever the occasion allowed.

After five years, we were transferred back to the United States. We moved to Roslyn, Virginia, just across the Key Bridge from Georgetown.

The Key Bridge, short for the Francis Scott Key Bridge, is a six-lane reinforced concrete arched bridge that crosses the Potomac River between the Rosslyn neighborhood of Arlington County, Virginia and the Georgetown neighborhood of Washington, D.C. The bridge was completed in 1923 and is Washington's oldest surviving bridge to cross the Potomac River.

Peter worked at Mobil Oil headquarters in Fairfax, Virginia. We traveled often to visit Mother and Heinz in New York. They still lived in the same apartment at 52 Arden Street in upper Manhattan.

Marianne was now seventy-two years old and remained spry. She still worked closely with the 34th Precinct and still fielded calls from those who needed assistance, or simply needed questions answered about available resources. Some of these people had witnessed robberies or violence but were hesitant to call the police. So, Mother did it for them. She called the 34th Precinct, relayed the details and filed reports where appropriate.

On one of the visits, we noticed that Mother was collecting a number of boxes from a well-known clearing house. I thought the boxes were a bit odd, since I'd never known her to order things from such places, but I chose to just let it be and didn't ask her about it.

While we were in Virginia, Heinz maintained the delicatessen and suffered an injury when a large money cash register fell and crushed his big toe. Despite the excruciating pain Heinz refused to go to the hospital for treatment since he felt that there was not much anyone could do for him.

The street life in New York City was rougher than anywhere else that we had lived. Once, when the boys were three or four years old, in the mid-1960's while on a visit to Oma and Opa's delicatessen, our son, Christopher, was outside of the deli and showing off to another young boy who seemed to be annoyed with Christopher. Opa watched through the large front window for a bit, then went to the door and called out, "Watch out, you'd better not do that!"

No sooner had the words come out of his mouth than the boy punched Christopher hard in the eye.

In 1991 Peter and I began thinking of our retirement and specifically what to do with all of our belongings in storage and in my mother's New York apartment. We knew that she would eventually need a place to live and our help with the day-to-day tasks. Her heart was no longer as strong as it had once been. Her doctor had recently reminded her of her two heart attacks.

In 1993, we purchased a second much larger house with three acres in Winter Haven, Florida. Since we were rarely able to stay in Florida, our eldest son and his family lived there to keep up the property. They also owned a smaller house which they rented out to save some money.

Often Heinz drove down to Florida to visit. He cooked and helped any way he could. Once in the early 90's, Christopher had killed a snake and placed it in the freezer to show the snake to Opa. While preparing dinner, Opa opened the freezer and nearly had a heart attack. He was pretty angry with Christopher but loved his grandchildren dearly.

Heinz (Opa) Hofmann and Christopher Hoverkamp

We also hired a housekeeper to come to the house every day to keep it clean. We retained the services of lawn and pest control personnel to keep the house in good condition. Peter and I paid all the necessary bills for the house. The big white house came with a guest house with a one bedroom apartment and a two-car garage. We expected the apartment would come in handy if and when my mother moved in. She could still keep her privacy and have us close by to help when needed.

We still had the first house on 110 Greenfield in a gated community on a golf course that we had purchased in 1984 when George and Kristy married and we were on our way to Saudi. Also, Christopher and Jacky and the family were living in that house.

Originally the boys lived there, while they attended college.

Eventually the day came when Heinz had had enough of trying to keep up with the deli, my mother, the 34th precinct, and New York City in general. Heinz felt exhausted and depressed. The deli had demanded all of his time, even on weekends.

The neighborhood had changed too much for his tastes. Gangs were increasing and too many folks simply loitered in the front of the deli. Many of his and mother's friends had moved away. He was afraid that there would be break-ins in their delicatessen. He just didn't like any of it. He decided to get rid of it.

Thinking back to when they sold the Deli, Marianne and Heinz purchased a large trailer with a living room, a king-size bed, bathroom, and a kitchenette. They attached the trailer to the back of their red Chevrolet. Neither of them had ever towed a trailer behind the car. I don't believe they realized the difficulty of backing up that big thing. They drove to our place in Yorktown Heights and had difficulty parking on our grass lot. I was so worried about them taking off on a big trip to drive from the East coast to California and back.

But off they went and they occasionally sent letters relating details of their trip and where they intended to drive next. Peter, the kids and I were amazed with how well they did. My parents had visited many of their German friends from Africa who now lived all across the States. Apparently they had a great time.

When they finished the trip, they parked that big trailer, of all places, in a nudist camp.

Later in 1993, Peter accepted another job in Doha Qatar.

Doha, the capital city of Qatar was home to nearly a half million people. Situated on the Persian Gulf, the city enjoys mild weather, though warm for my taste. This however, was a welcome relief after

leaving

Opa and Heidi Hoverkamp

Norway.

Once around 1987 mother visited us in Jeddah, Saudi Arabia and while she was there she felt strong enough to go sightseeing. During her stay, she decided that she wanted to ride a camel. We did some research and found a likely place that gave camel rides to tourists.

The tourist attraction was a sand filled dust bowl that, I imagine, gave the camels plenty of room to roam. The owner of the small business, a stereotypical Arab man, dressed in traditional clothing, the dishdasha (robe), and Abayah (head cover). The man was gracious and, I suspect, quite taken with mother. He picked a particularly gentle camel for her.

Mother mounted the camel while it was lying down and found a comfortable sitting position. But when the camel stood up, she was terrified. Still, she held tight and protested only through facial expressions, and went for a short walk while riding the camel. Later she told us that she enjoyed the ride immensely.

We ate dinners with a few of the Saudies and watched some traditional dances. She bought a few trinkets and enjoyed bargaining with the merchants. I explained to her when they name a price, cut that price in half and watch their reactions. I had learned this technique in Indonesia.

After two weeks she returned to New York. Opa picked her up and soon she was back on duty in the New York neighborhood. The 34th precinct continued to award her for her neighborhood cleanup efforts and she was always proud of them.

I was concerned one night, however, when Mother called in the middle of the night. She somehow had become convinced that she had won the clearinghouse contest and was now wealthy. Of course, she soon found she was mistaken. I began to wonder how much of their money she had been spending on these trinkets.

In 1996, Peter and I left Doha, Qatar for Winter Haven, Florida as Peter was going to retire. He had had a heart attack while we were on home leave in June of 1995 and returned to work four weeks later. We felt however that if he had another event it would be best of we were in the U.S. so we decided to retire in 1996. We hoped to have a permanent home base for a change. Little did we know that having a home base didn't mean our lives would settle down. My mother eventually moved more slowly and seemed more tired. She began to get overwhelmed and soon, depression set in. The 34th precinct remained kind to her and patient because she could be a little headstrong when she wanted something done in her neighborhood.

Unfortunately, during our separation, Heinz had been diagnosed with colon cancer. Mother called late one evening to share the news. The doctors said that he needed radiation and chemo treatments to stand any chance of beating the disease. Mother fussed and fumed that she did not agree with chemo, she would agree only to the radiation treatments; she feared Heinz would lose his beautiful wavy hair.

During Heinz's treatments, somehow in trying to save him, they had increased the radiation doses and I'm convinced they had over radiated him. One after another, his organs turned black. He required a colonoscopy bag which he carried on his left side. My mother and I often helped him change the bag and clean everything out as needed. Heinz suffered severe pain.

Doctors and nurses believed that Heinz must have removed the urine bag at some point and the poison from his urine had quickly spread throughout his body. There was no medical treatment that could help him any longer.

It broke my heart to see this once vibrant and lively man dwindle away to bones. He'd lost the playful sparkle in his eye. The smile that once came so easily now seemed forced, and then only in his best moments.

My mother was one brave lady at this time when Heinz needed her so very much.

MARIANNE HOFMANN WITH MAYOR ED KOCH

CHAMBER OF COMMERE DINNER
SEPT. 25, 1971
CAPT. ANDERSON, CLARENCE SWEEN, TOM O'BRIEN
NEW YORK 34TH PRECINCT

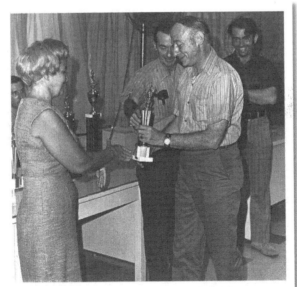

MARIANNE PRESENTING AWARDS AT
CHAMBER OF COMMERCE CEREMONY

Marianne speaking at awards dinner

Marianne with Mayor Koch

## Chapter 16

On October 26, 1992, Mother and I stood over Opa's bed when he neared the end. We were still living in Rosslyn (Arlington), Virginia. The doctor had administered strong doses of morphine to ease his pain, leaving him semiconscious but aware of our presence. He closed his eyes, and smiled slightly. His final breath exhaled in a soft sigh and then he was gone. Despite his lifeless body, his comforting spirit remained around us for several moments before the room emptied.

Heinrich Hofmann, our Opa who had gently but surely carved his place into our lives and our hearts, had gone. When someone close to us passes away, it is with some sadness and effort that we realize we must allow them to move on. At the same time, we were grateful to see Opa's suffering end.

The funeral for Heinz Hofmann was held in a church near their apartment and delicatessen. The New York Police Department honored him with their presence and dozens of friends came to pay their respects and offer condolences. Many expressed their feelings for Heinz as a kind and caring man, which echoed our sentiments for Opa. Our family still misses him very much.

Something in Opa's passing triggered a hoarding instinct in my mother. Before, of course, I had noticed several boxes from the clearinghouse, and now the packages all addressed to Mother in bold, black letters, seemed to arrive by the truckload. Each package contained an advertisement that claimed that she could be the "largest winner ever" if she simply purchased this item or that, or spent another 'X' amount of dollars. I found it difficult to believe that my mother had fallen into this trap to purchase in order to win. Numerous unopened boxes taunted me with the black and white, bold lettering bearing her name and address.

Mother continued to buy, hoping for that big win. She spent the majority of the life savings that she and Heinz had worked so hard to squirrel away for their future.

My heart broke each time I walked through the apartment, squeezing between the unopened boxes that were stacked in rows, leaving little room for passage. I couldn't see how she could ever store all of this stuff, much less clean the apartment to resemble the neatness she'd always advocated. With each new delivery, mother would stack higher, or pull and push stacks of boxes to make room for more. Eventually the stacks reached the ceiling and I was uncertain what she might do next.

With Heinz's death, the constant delivery of packages, and trying to pay the bills, Mother became stressed. So stressed that she required medication and eventually was hospitalized. Mother, unpredictable as always, became unruly and had to be restrained. The doctor eventually phoned me and demanded that I pick her up within the week, or they would confiscate her money and all of her belongings and put her in a nursing home.

Fortunately, I had another good doctor friend to consult. He advised that I pick her up immediately and let the staff know, in no uncertain terms, that their treatment of my mother was shameful and unprofessional. I had been in such a quandary with what to do with her that his words seemed, in an odd sense, to give me permission. Permission to unload the guilt I had felt over my mother and how she had been treated, back onto the hospital staff. I drove to that hospital in a rage. I don't doubt that the staff sensed my wrath when I hit the doors.

After raining hell down on the doctor and hospital staff, I brought Mother back to the apartment and began to sift through her belongings. During the day I took care of her, at night I dragged boxes of her unneeded belongings to the elevator door and then in the early mornings I hauled it down to the street to wait for the city garbage truck to come and take it away. She, on the other hand, gathered papers and documents that she no longer needed, and shredded them. We found thousands of lottery tickets; stacks of lost dreams bundled in rubber bands. She had cubby holes and hidden compartments in the apartment ceiling, and hidden slide doors to secrete her jewelry. Several boxes were filled with rolled pennies, taken from the Deli in hopes that at least one may be worth big money one day. She had a large jar that could hold five gallons of liquid, but she had filled it with quarters. We eventually gave all of the pennies to our housekeepers and the quarters to Peter's brother, Fred.

While pulling one of the boxes from the ceiling, they all came down knocking me off the ladder. Mother had quite a laugh over that, and I joined in her laughter once my bruised behind healed somewhat.

During my stay I also learned that the clearinghouse wasn't the only questionable business extorting money from my mother. She had received a couple of phone calls that I casually listened to, and soon realized that something wasn't right. When I asked about it, she was evasive.

I listened in on one such conversation from the hall phone while she spoke on the phone in her bedroom. The call was from some fortune telling company, of all things! The person on the other end was quite rude and forceful, demanding that she send them money immediately. I broke in on the conversation, telling him who I was and that they would stop calling her immediately, or they would hear from our attorney. Oddly, whenever I answered future calls, the caller often hung up. Still, when she answered, I imagined what they were saying on the other end. I was so disturbed that I hung up the phone for her.

In speaking with the local postal officials, they advised that everyone should return packages and letters from companies like the clearinghouse or the fortune tellers, unopened. I simply wrote on the letters and packages, "Return to Sender" and tried to forget they had ever arrived. Still, I dreaded what would happen once I left Mother alone.

When we had cleaned the clutter from the dwelling, Peter arranged for a moving truck to pack up her furniture and move it into a rented storage unit. Eventually, we hoped, she would sort out the remainder to either bring to our Florida guesthouse, or donate to charity. All of this was traumatic for Mother and exhausted me. Peter became anxious for me to return to him and the family.

One day in 1997 when Peter and I next visited New York City, Mother wanted desperately to go to E 86th St. which is the old Germantown area. We drove her to *Schaller and Weber* a large and well known German food shop to purchase some of the food she liked.

When we left the shop, she mentioned that she felt good. As we crossed 3rd Ave. and 86th Street, she passed out; just collapsed onto the street and fell into a mud puddle. Her skin was pale. When Peter knelt over her and said that she wasn't breathing, my heart stopped.

Then, Peter said, "I think she is gone."

I shook my head and blurted, "No! She can't die here in the middle of the street and in the mud, no!"

Then, I added, "Peter you press on her chest and I'll breathe into her mouth. Neither Peter nor I had ever performed C.P.R. before, but we knew the general idea. While Peter pumped her chest and I delivered her breaths, I noticed her color return and an actual line of pink moved across her face and upward. We continued for about eight to ten minutes, though it seemed longer. During this time a passerby called the Fire and Rescue squad and they came quickly!

The paramedics took over and then carted her off to the hospital. When she arrived at Lenox Hospital, she was breathing on her own but would need a long recovery. Recently her doctor had told us that she occasionally experienced small heart attacks and had suffered some severe damage to her heart. I had never taken him seriously until now.

Mother remained in the hospital while they conducted tests and determined that her heart was weak and out of rhythm.. While there, we had a serious talk about her moving to Florida with us. She declined saying she was too much of a city girl. Mother and I differed in that respect, as well as many others, I suppose. It may have stemmed from my time on the farm with Romy and the Ackermann's but I always preferred the quiet of the country. Mother's spirit soared in the hustle and action of the city. She fed on the noise, and at times the turmoil of city life.

Despite her refusal, shortly after I brought her home I flew back to Florida to prepare the guest house. Even if she didn't understand it, I knew it was only a matter of time now before Mother would come to live with us.

Mother had made a good friend in her neighbor lady who kept an eye on her, and assured me that she would call me immediately should anything happen.

Mother's furniture was delivered to storage in Florida and Peter and I flew her to Florida with us. While she technically lived with us, she maintained her own little apartment in the guest house. The place was comfortable, providing all she needed and she had her family around her. Funny, we had installed an intercom like you have with a newborn baby in the family so that we could hear her if anything happened and she needed help at night. However, she was just as feisty as ever!

Even though her grandchildren, Kelsey, Asheton and Katelyn often spent time with her, we suspected she wouldn't be happy there for long. We soon moved her to a garden apartment geared more for people her age. We moved all of her things in to give her that 'homey' feeling. The apartment was only five minutes away from our house.

I believe she truly tried to like living there but she was not happy. Soon, she simply gave up and became very ill. Her heart was not strong enough anymore.

# Epilogue

At the age of seventy-nine, Mother passed away on January 31, 1997 in the Winter Haven Hospital at 7:00 A.M. Later, a nurse mentioned to me that it had been a blessing that she had passed so quickly. She had seen many of the elderly suffer for long periods before they passed.

The funeral was held at a local funeral parlor. Mother wore her favorite blue dress that she often wore during the police department functions, meetings with Mayor Koch or other New York City officials.

We found some irony in her funeral after announcing her passing in the local newspapers. Many of the folks she had known in New York attended the funeral. Apparently, many of them had moved from New York and now lived locally. I believe if she had met them in Florida earlier, she may have found some happiness in her final days.

All that my Mother, Marianne Jerke Krankemann-Hofmann, was or ever hoped to be, she found in the city of New York and in the eyes of her grandchildren. Grandchildren offer us a second chance through their innocence. New York City had offered her a chance to face her demons, and to eventually overcome them, strengthen and to blossom.

I think we all show our good and bad sides at some point in life. Perhaps Mother took both sides to the extreme but it's not for me to judge. I have my own thoughts about her and those thoughts will remain mine alone.

I don't doubt that Heinz recognized her goodness or he wouldn't have tolerated her antics for so many years. Of one thing I am certain; life with Mother was never monotonous. Heinz was a strong man in many ways, a product of his war years, I imagine. His strength bolstered my mother and allowed her to shine.

Our daughter Heidi now has the tapestry that Heinz's late wife crafted in her final days. The tapestry hangs on her dining room wall and I am always amazed by it. The tapestry clearly shows two large cranes erecting the Köln Dome. I'm astounded that she crafted the piece depicting the Dome with a simple sewing machine.

I never saw Romy again, though I still think of her occasionally. I still miss Viktor and Patch and our walks or cow rides at sunset.

Marga and I remain best friends. I am truly blessed to have grown through life with her to always depend on. Since we reconnected in 1977 we have visited Fuessen with our children and eventually our grandchildren (all fifteen of us) at least once a year and often two or three times a year depending on where we were living. We know that this year, 2013, that as our family grows and multiplies and work schedules are diverse, we won't be able to continue this any longer. Of course our advancing years also have an impact on this practice. However, this cross-country experience has been heartwarming for Peter and I as we hear our kids, (Kids! 52, 51, and 45 years old!) and grandkids talk about their most recent visit to Fuessen. They talk of the things they did with Marga's kids and grandchildren and how much they look forward to their next visit. Marga and I speak almost weekly by phone about the things grandmothers (Oma's) do!

Mother's scrap books hold the newspaper clippings from every major daily newspaper in New York City of the Madison Square garden event. To the day she passed she remained steadfastly proud of the work she had done for the citizens of New York, and rightly so.

I've come to believe that we are born to life to make a difference in the world, no matter how small that difference may be. I don't know if Marianne Hofmann shared this belief, but she carried out the mission with a vengeance.

It seems a shame that we learn our most valuable lessons in our twilight years. And those lessons are the simple ones; cherish family, always. Yes, we may not always agree but this is often what makes life interesting and endears us to those we love.

I've also learned that when we have a chance to travel, we have a chance to broaden our horizon. Never look back. Always clean up where you are staying before you go to bed at night. Lay out your clothes the night before for the next day, you never know what the night will bring.

Never talk negatively about yourself to anyone. Hold your head high.

If you have a family, most importantly, keep a good routine. Always check out what your children say; listen to them but check later to see if what they tell you is true.

In one way or another, I learned much of this wisdom from my mother. Although, Marianne Jerke Krankemann-Hofmann, was often erratic and unpredictable, she was and always will be my mother. For this, I am grateful.

### 

The End

## ABOUT THE AUTHOR

Christel E. Hoverkamp was born in Berlin, Germany. After fleeing Germany, she moved to the United States. Her subsequent travels have led her to reside in England, Indonesia, Norway, Saudi Arabia and Qatar.

Ms. Hoverkamp deeply loves her family and friends. Her interests include writing, fishing, golf, tennis, gardening, practicing speaking German, Indonesian, Arabic and most recently, Chinese.

She now resides in Florida with her husband, Peter and has written and published a second book, *Executive Moves: Life of an Executive Wife*.

Frank Redding
(703) 780-8055

Made in the USA
Middletown, DE
29 November 2020

25659137R00097